Machu Picchu's Sacred Sisters: Choquequirao and Llactapata

Astronomy, Symbolism, and Sacred Geography in the Inca Heartland

Gary R. Ziegler
J. McKim Malville

Johnson Books
BOULDER

Published by Johnson Books, a Big Earth Publishing company
3005 Center Green Drive, Suite 225
Boulder, Colorado 80301
1-800-258-5830
E-mail: books@bigearthpublishing.com
www.bigearthpublishing.com

Cover and text design by D. Kari Luraas
Cover photo: Overview of the lower and upper plaza groups taken from the *usnu* hill. Lillian Roberts photo.

9 8 7 6 5 4 3 2 1

ISBN: 978-1-55566-457-2
Library of Congress Control Number: 2013953420

Please Note: Risk is always a factor in backcountry and high-mountain travel. Many of the activities described in this book can be dangerous, especially when weather is adverse or unpredictable, and when unforeseen events or conditions create a hazardous situation. The authors have done their best to provide the reader with accurate information about backcountry travel, as well as to point out some of its potential hazards. It is the responsibility of the users of this guide to learn the necessary skills for safe backcountry travel, and to exercise caution in potentially hazardous areas. The authors and publisher disclaim any liability for injury or other damage caused by backcountry traveling or performing any other activity described in this book.

Printed in the United States of America

For Percy Paz,
insatiable researcher and Andean explorer
who dedicated his life to unraveling
the secrets of Choquequirao and the Incas

Contents

Foreword

By John Hemming
Former Director
of the Royal Geographical Society

This book, *Machu Picchu's Sacred Sisters: Choquequirao and Llactapata,* is the right book at the right time and by the right people. Peru's tourism authorities have for years been promoting Choquequirao as an alternative to Machu Picchu. They hope that this "sacred sister" will take pressure off that world-famous site, which is drowning under the flood of visitors. In recent years, many discoveries have been made in and around Choquequirao, and its archaeological survey and restoration are now largely complete. So this is just the right moment for an accessible book in English about this beautiful and fascinating Inca royal estate.

It is often forgotten that during the century before Hiram Bingham's sensational discoveries in 1911, Choquequirao was believed to have been Manco Inca's lost city of Vilcabamba. This was what brought the French diplomat, Eugène de Lavandais, Vicomte de Sartiges, there in 1834; followed by another French diplomat and artist, Léonce Angrand, a decade later. Peru's greatest geographer, Antonio Raimondi, never quite reached Choquequirao, but he was sure that it was Manco's Vilcabamba. Other adventurers got there (or claimed that they had) and the Limeño historian Carlos Romero made a serious study of the ruin.

It was Romero and a treasure-hunting local *alcalde* who persuaded Hiram Bingham to go there in 1909. This was Bingham's first sight of a remote Inca ruin. He made a fine survey of the site; his enthusiasm about it fired up his Yale classmates to finance the 1911 expedition, and the rest is history. So, ironically, it was Choquequirao that led to the discovery of the far larger and more glamorous lost city that eclipsed it.

Gary Ziegler and Kim Malville are the right people to author this book. Gary himself made some of the discoveries—he has been in the field with Hugh Thomson and Vincent Lee, he has worked with and admires Percy Paz and the other archaeologists, he has read all the literature, and he has tramped and mapped every Inca road around the site. As an astronomer, Kim Malville adds a very important dimension by showing how often Inca sites are aligned to astronomical events and sacred sightlines. Both authors are foot soldiers, so they relate buildings, waterworks, terracing, roads, and platforms to the terrain. This gives greater understanding of the Incas' close identity with Pachamama, mother earth, and their veneration as *huacas* (sacred place) of mountains, rocks, caves, and springs.

Llactapata, the other "sacred sister" in this book, is very different than Choquequirao. First noted by Bingham, who briefly visited one of the groups and rediscovered in part by David Drew in the early 1980s, Llactapata was thoroughly explored and surveyed by Gary Ziegler and Hugh Thomson in 2003. With Kim Malville, the astrophysicist on the team, and using new techniques of remote sensing, exciting discoveries were made to link this sacred place to Machu Picchu, which is visible on the next mountain spur.

This book is about more than these two fascinating sites. It gives a lively look at a rugged, spectacular, and highly important—but little-known—part of the Inca empire.

Introduction

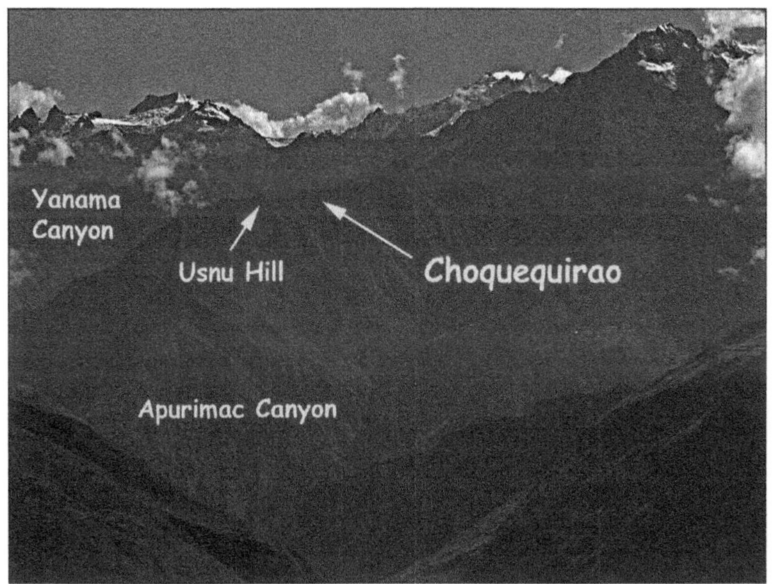

Distant view of Choquequirao from the road to Huanipaca. G. Ziegler photo.

We began this writing as a monograph intended for a conference on archeoastronomy to be held in Lima during January 2011. It soon became evident that much more deserved to be included from the vast collection of files, photos, and field notes accumulated over years of work at and around Choquequirao by ourselves and dedicated colleagues. The result is that we have expanded and broadened the content to present a more interesting and readable work with appeal to the informed non-academic reader, interested traveler, and professional Andean scholar.

We discuss the importance of sacred features and *huacas* at

Machu Picchu, Choquequiro, and other regional sites along with the story of the exciting rediscovery and ceremonial significance of Hiram Bingham's lost Llactapata. Stories and notes from expedition journals are interspersed with soundly researched and referenced facts, data, and qualified interpretation. The result is a diagram-intensive book that we hope conveys the excitement and adventure of extreme archaeology in the cloud-forested Andes, along with an understanding of remarkable Inca accomplishments and appreciation for Choquequirao, an important, enigmatic, spectacular Andean Inca city, rivaling in many ways its famous sister site, Machu Picchu.

We provide a summary history and description of this unique Inca royal estate, carefully constructed high on a narrow ridge above the Apurimac River in a remote region of the Peruvian Andes. We conclude that Choquequirao was built as a royal estate during the late fifteenth century by the Inca ruler, Topa Inca Yupanki, and modeled after Machu Picchu with relationship to sacred geography and cosmic alignment. It was built in part by workers imported from Chachapoyas in northern Peru during the height of imperial expansion.

Choquequirao has alignments with the June and December solstices, suggesting a strong solar ceremonial focus and year-round ceremonial activities. A large truncated hill served as an *usnu*—a ceremonial platform and celestial-terrestrial observatory. We suggest the site may have provided a regional ceremonial and pilgrimage destination during imperial times. Choquequirao appears to have been occupied during early colonial years by the last neo-Inca and was abandoned shortly before or after the death of the last tutelar Inca, Tupac Amaru, in 1572.

One
Location and History

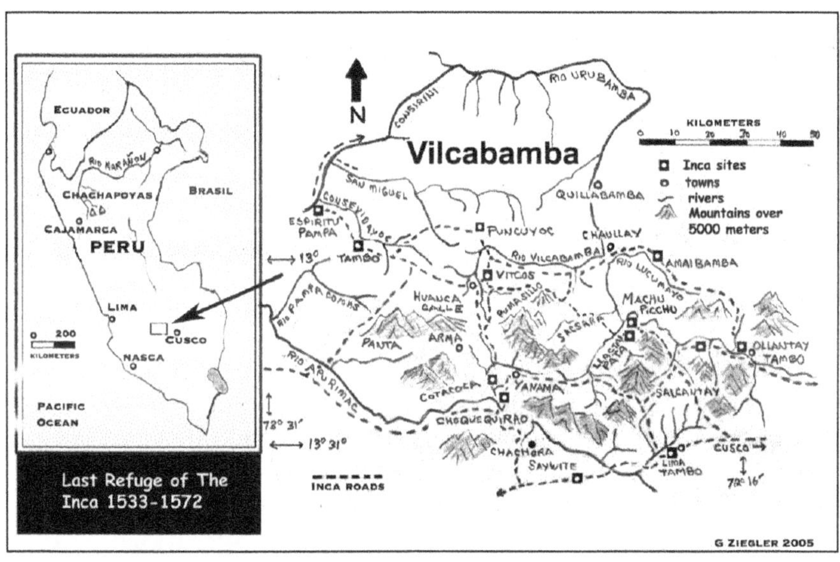

Map diagram of the Vilcabamba region. G. Ziegler diagram.

The Choquequirao archaeological complex is situated at 9,800 feet elevation on a southwest facing spur of a glaciated 17,716-foot peak leading down to the deep Apurimac River canyon at 4,900 feet. The site is 61 miles west of Cusco in the rugged, cloud-forest covered, remote Vilcabamba range of the Peruvian Andes.

Prehistory

Information about life before the Inca in the Vilcabamba region is sparse, as few studies have been conducted. Many ridges and hilltops in the habitable zone, up to 13,000 feet elevation, contain remnants of round foundation settlements. Circular,

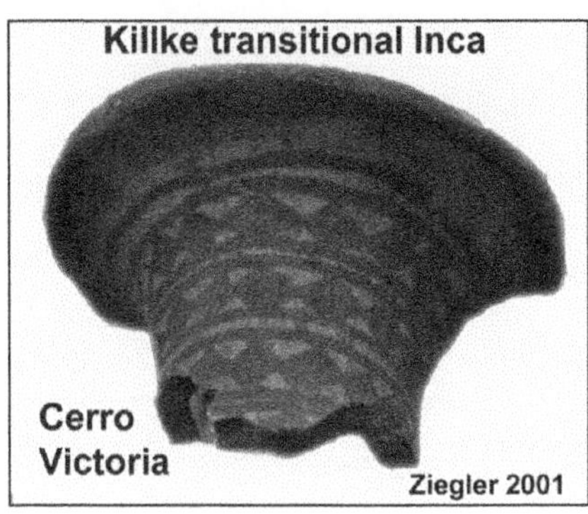

Image of Killke-style pottery fragment from Cerro Victoria. G. Ziegler photo.

sub-surface, stone-lined burial chambers are common.[1] As Inca administrators took over regional control and the threat of attack was lessened, settlements moved down to more hospitable lower ground. This however, was rarely possible in the steep Vilcabamba (Kendall 1984).

Inca legend, promoted by the surviving descendant clan, or *panaca*, of the Inca ruler Pachacuti conveyed a version of Inca history to Spanish chroniclers according to which the Inca expanded into the Vilcabamba in the mid-1400s following the defeat of a rival polity, the *Chanca*, under Pachacuti's inspired leadership (Betanzos 1968). The archaeological record does not support this. Excavations at Corihuayrachina (Cerro Victoria, *cerro* meaning mountain) near Choquequirao in 2001 recovered Killke-type early Inca transitional pottery from burials there, suggesting much earlier regional Inca occupation (Ziegler 2001).

It appears that the Inca were organized as an advancing state well before the mid-fifteenth century. The earlier Huari-Tiahuanaco cultural expansion had peaked and died some four hundred years before Pachacuti's ascendancy to the Inca throne. A return to unsettled times with small, competing chiefdoms and regional strife, a sort of Andean dark ages followed. One of these chiefdoms in the southern highlands of Peru evolved to become the expanding Inca state (Bauer 1992; D'Altroy 2003). The property of the ruling Inca became the holding of his *panaca* (kinship group) following his death.

Each successive Inca built his own estates and monuments. The Inca Huayna Capac established a second capital in Ecuador during the early 1500s. It is now generally accepted that Machu Picchu was designed and construction started as a royal estate and ceremonial center by the Inca Pachacuti (Rowe 1990). The nearby Vilcabamba region must have been under Inca control sometime before this. The Vilcabamba is known somewhat romantically as "the last refuge of the Inca." Dismembered by epidemic disease and protracted civil war, the empire collapsed in 1533 with the capture and later execution of the Inca Athahualpa by Spanish invaders.

Three years later, in 1536, Manco, a son of Huayna Capac who had been appointed ruling Inca by the Spanish after the death of Athahualpa, escaped his handlers to stage a massive rebellion that almost recaptured Peru. When the siege eventually failed, Manco, with a part of the army, followers, and what remained of Inca leadership, retreated into the remote Vilcabamba. Manco's captains and sons maintained a neo-Inca mini-state until 1572, when Manco's last remaining son, Tupac Amaru, was captured in the remote lower jungle beyond Vilcabamba and executed in Cusco (Hemming 1993).

Late neo-Inca plate and miniature pot from Choquequirao. G. Ziegler photo.

Archaeological evidence indicates that Choquequirao was originally built during imperial times and was occupied at some time during the late neo-Inca state. Locally made, colonial-influenced pottery, as well as earlier classic imperial style, is found around the site (COPESCO 1987; Samanez 1995). Some walls, windows, and walkways have been filled suggesting that later occupants may have considered limiting access, possibly for defense.

Imperial Inca-style pot fragments from Choquequirao. G. Ziegler photo.

Evidence from excavation indicates that the entire complex of structures was burned not long after abandonment. The charred remains of roof supports and cross members indicate the fire occurred before the wood had time to decay. We can only speculate about when and why this happened. As with Machu Picchu, we probably will never know the precise time and reason for abandonment.[2]

The large, two-story, gabled residences and high status, double-jamb entranceways are similar to Machu Picchu and

(Top) The Elite Residence and *kallanca* from the lower plaza of Choquequirao. G. Ziegler photo. (Left) Double-jamb entrance to the Elite Residence group before clearing. Hugh Thomson photo. (Right) Image of the double-jamb entranceway to the *usnu* hill. Paolo Greer photo.

Topa Inca's royal estate at Chinchero (Lee 1998). French anthropologist Erwan Duffait presents evidence from early colonial documents that the region was claimed by Topa Inca's kinship group, or *panaca* (Duffait 2005). Topa Inca succeeded Pachacuti during the late 1400s. We propose that Choquequirao was constructed at this time.

The two principal administrative residential centers associated with neo-Inca Vilcabamba, Vitcos and Vilcabamba (the city, referred to as La Vieja), have historical reference having been visited by outsiders.[3] Colonial armies raided Vitcos and Vilcabamba. Manco's son, Titu Cusi, became the Inca ruler after Manco's death in 1544. He dictated his memoirs describing events and places in the region (Titu Cusi 1570). However, no historical reference has been found referring to the more impressive Choquequirao or any place like it. Metal items, horseshoes, and Spanish-style roofing tiles have been found at Vilcabamba. Similar items were found at Vitcos (Hemming 1993; Lee 2000; Savoy 1970). Nothing of Spanish origin has been reported from Choquequirao (COPESCO 1987; Duffait 2005; Ziegler 1999).

History

Choquequirao was first reported by a prospector, Juan Arias Diaz Topete, in 1710. Several others, including the French diplomat Eugene de Sartiges, reached Choquequirao during the next century. Excellent drawings and a partial site map were made by another French diplomat, Léonce Angrand, in 1847. The site was indicated on several early regional maps. The first mapping and survey was conducted by a party led by Hiram Bingham in February 1909 (Bingham 1910; Lee 1998; Ziegler 1999).

Choquequirao was then largely ignored until the Peruvian government showed interest in the late 1980s. Fewer than a hundred visitors were recorded to have reached the site since Bingham.[4] In 1986, a preliminary study of Choquequirao was conducted for the government by the Peruvian architect Roberto Samanez (Samanez 1995). In 1992, a government restoration, preservation, and investigation project by the agency COPESCO, directed by the Peruvian archaeologist Percy Paz, was started. The project continues as of this writing.

In 2002, the Inca road that afforded the only access to Choquequirao was located and documented by the Royal

Geographical Society–supported Andean Research Expedition, led by Ziegler and British author and explorer Hugh Thomson while investigating an associated site, Cotacoca, in the deep Yanama Canyon.[5] (Thomson 2006; Ziegler 2002).

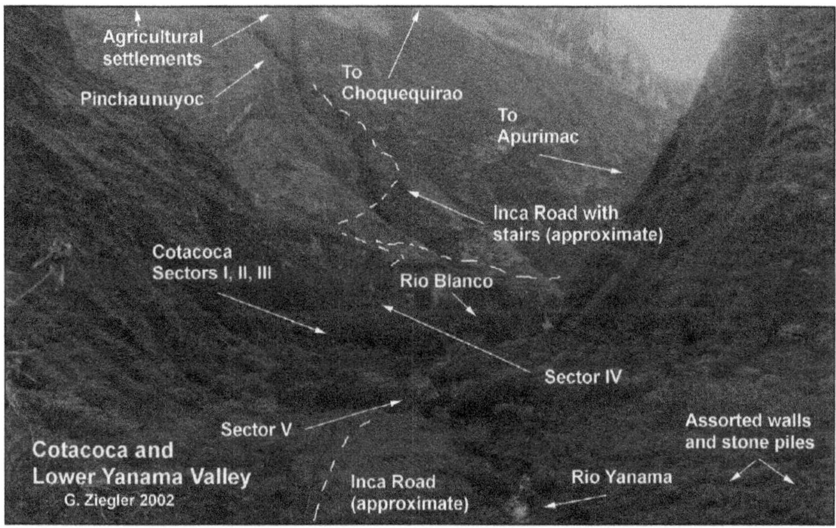

Image of the Yanama Valley and Cotacoca. G. Ziegler diagram.

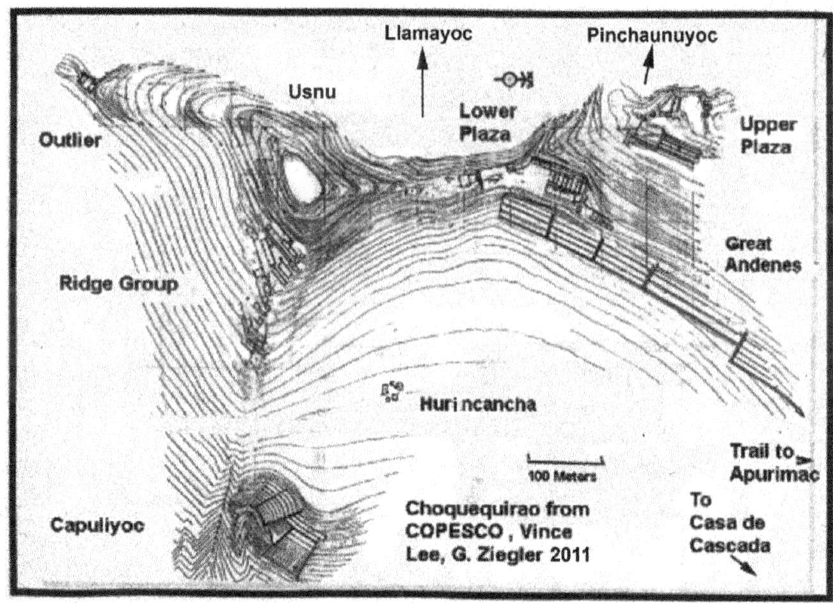

Site plan of Choquequirao. Percy Paz, Vince Lee, and G. Ziegler diagram.

Percy Paz, assisted by others over the years, including American architect Vincent Lee and Gary Ziegler, had compiled extensive data and a large collection of cultural material: tools, ceramics, and burial accoutrements, which are cataloged and stored in Cusco. The principal features and structures at Choquequirao have been cleared of vegetation, with many reconstructed or reinforced.[6] Continuing exploration of the difficult, steep, cloud-forest covered terrain has revealed terraces, the original canal bringing water to the site, unique rock art, and other outlying structures.

Measurements and photos taken by Bingham and his associate, Clarence Hay, in 1909 produced the first site map and a reasonable topographic chart of the surrounding terrain. We now have a complete site plan to work with. Incorporating data from the Samanez study, Percy Paz and team completed a very accurate site survey supplemented by aerial photos, a modern topographic map, and GPS positioning. As of this writing, low-resolution satellite imagery is available free online from Google Earth.

Notes

Hugh Thomson (l.) and Gary Ziegler (r). Hugh Thomson photo.

1. We have examined many of these sites throughout the Vilcabamba, which we believe are pre-Inca *Chanca* settlements. No documented regional excavation seems to have taken place except at the Cusicaca project sites west of Ollantaytambo. In 2001, Cusco archaeologist Alfredo Valencia and Gary Ziegler excavated several round structures and tombs at Cerro Victoria (Corihuayrachina). We believe these were settlements of agricultural

workers under Inca administration. *Chanca* sites are well known and extensively documented beyond the Vilcabamba at Abancay, Huancavalica, and the lower Apurimac.

Ziegler Field Notes 1999: Corihuayrachina

Hugh Thomson and I pulled ourselves up the final 10 feet to mount a narrow ledge that led straight to the top of the ridge. The view of the ice peaks and surrounding valleys was magnificent. We were making our way along the top of the ridge, still intending to scout the potential platform site on the next mountain, when we realized that the crest of the ridge was lined with tombs. So … with climbing rope, sharpened machetes, and great enthusiasm, we embarked to scale the mountain. With some difficulty we reached the described ridge. When someone said narrow he was not kidding! Halfway along the knife-edge ridge we came upon a 1.5-foot wide fieldstone wall capping the ridge, which dropped vertically some 160 feet on both sides.

Dicey going indeed … we crab-walked across to reach the widening approach to the summit. I could see the remnants of what was a very airy walkway leading across the ridge to the conical top above us. As a climber of some experience, I am not easily intimidated by heights, but this must have been challenging for anyone carrying bodies or offerings up here, something I would not consider attempting. At this point, Hollywood would have had Harrison Ford dangling from the end of a rope held by the heroine as a deadly bushmaster slithers onto her ledge!

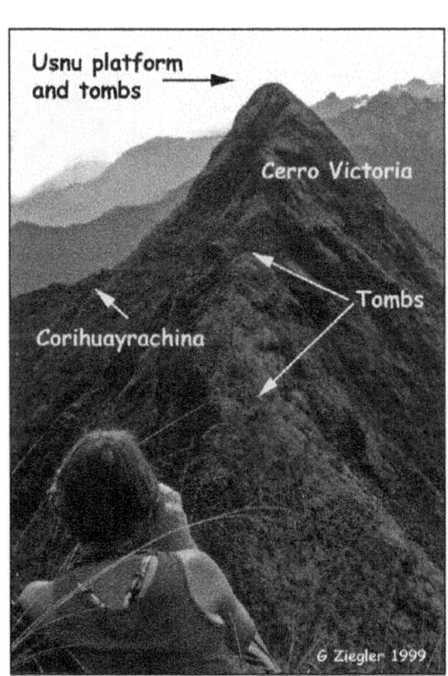

Corihuayrachina and Cerro Victoria. G. Ziegler photo.

Arriving on top we are not surprised that the view is exceptional in all directions. Several jug-shaped holes dot the crest along with the remains of round foundations or platforms. Several more slightly raised mounds indicate that perhaps all had not been looted. We poke around a bit with machetes, but find nothing to indicate who the builders may have been. I feel that this site is very similar to the hilltop remains on the way to Yanama, probably dating from the same time. Johan Reinhard mentions that he has seen similar mountaintop sites that were Inca. He says that the chambers may well contain offerings and not necessarily bodies.

The following year, 2000, Peter Frost submitted a proposal to *National Geographic*, which resulted in a grant to investigate the Cerro Victoria–Corihuayrachina area. In 2001, Peter, Cusco archaeologist Alfredo Vallencia, and I returned with excavating and surveying teams and a film crew in tow to investigate what we hoped was a major Inca complex linked to Choquequirao. Extensive exploration revealed a large scattered assortment of simple round structures, a small Inca administrative center and an abnormally large number of individual burial tombs. Unfortunately, most were looted, but we did recover a profusion of Inca-period pot shards and to our surprise, some examples of early Killke—Inca transition pottery.

We concluded that the region probably served as a bedroom community for workers involved in mining the nearby San Juan silver deposits and as an extensive agriculture-producing area in support of Choquequirao. With the exception of a sacred *usnu* platform on the summit of Cerro Victoria, we could not identify other ceremonial structures. We did discover the following year, during the RGS-supported Cotacoca exploration, that the main Inca road from Yanama passed below through Cotacoca along the Yanama River, then up through Pinchaunuyoc to Choquequirao.

2. Ziegler Field Notes 1996: Residence Group

The excavation carefully peeled back the layers of accumulated organic debris, digging down through soil and clay to the base of the original floor in several of the buildings. The lowest level is a hard packed clay—the original floor. Over this is a thin layer of dirt, followed by a thicker layer of charcoal. This layer contains the identifiably burned residue of heavy wood timbers and smaller rounded poles, which we believe are the remains of the original roof. We conclude that the dirt layer represents a brief period of abandonment followed by a fire that destroyed the burnable portions of the buildings.

This creates yet another mystery. The place was abandoned, then a short time later, a year or more perhaps, the buildings were destroyed by fire. It could not have been much longer. My observation is that pole and thatch roofs at this elevation and climate do not last more than a couple of years. My first thought was that a wildfire, common in the area, had swept through part of the site. However, Percy Paz says that every structure he has examined in different sectors shows the same occurrence. The sectors are distant from each other and some are separated by ridges. It would have been unlikely that a natural fire could have reached every sector. We conclude that Choquequirao was deliberately and systematically burned shortly after its abandonment. So ... another mystery in this place of mysteries ... After the last Inca shut the door and turned out the lights, who came back and torched the place and why?

After the last Inca, Tupac Amaru's, capture in the jungles beyond Espiritu Pampa [Vilcabamba], did a holdout band of Inca captains return to destroy the holy city before it could be defiled by Spanish colonials? We know that the Inca burned Vilcabamba as they fled from the approaching Spanish army. Or, did the Spanish themselves, as part of a policy to eradicate further Inca insurrection, burn Choquequirao? Neither theory seems likely. No evidence has been found that the Spanish ever visited the area or knew of its existence. History is silent on the subject. Except

for the fire, Choquequirao, like its sister estate, Machu Picchu, was abandoned with it walls and temples largely undamaged by human hand.

John Hemming and Vince Lee both doubt that the neo-Inca occupied Choquequirao. Hemming reasonably points out that there should be some historical reference as there is for Vitcos and Vilcabamba (La Vieja). John writes in personal communication: "That Vince Lee and I think that any colonial artifacts found there by Percy Paz would have been from when it was part of the post-conquest *encomienda* of Urcos and would thus have been at the edge of Spanish Peru far earlier than 1572. The Augustinian missionaries in Vilcabamba in the 1560s never bothered with that area south of Vilcabamba. Had it been part of the Manco fiefdom, they would have wanted to build a church there. Also, the armed contingents that entered Vilcambamba from the west in 1572 from Abancay and from Guamanga (Ayacucho) crossed the Apurimac at Osambre (Cusambi) and up the Arma River—but did not go near Choquequirao, presumably because the Inca had no presence there at that time."

Late Inca pottery from Choquequirao. Percy Paz diagram.

This brings up an intriguing divergence of two opinions, both with credibility. The strongest argument is that there is no historical reference to Choquequirao. However, the archaeological evidence supports the view that the last Inca were there at some time, if only briefly. Percy categorized the recovered pottery as Type C (colonial) but Vilcabamba style, which was made from clay containing much locally metamorphic mica. No glazed examples or colonial metal items have been found there, which would be expected if it had been occupied during the early colonial years as an *encomienda*. I can find no mention of a place like Choquequirao in the documents pertaining to Urcos or from an *encomienda* centered at Cochora. Erwan Duffait in his "Choquequirao en el siglo XVI: etnohistoria e implicaciones arqueologicas," Bulletin de l'Institut d'Etudes Andines 34:185–196, makes a weak argument for Choquequirao as part of an early colonial period *encomienda*.

A unique aspect of Choquequirao is that it apparently had no access from the southern, Apurimac side, only from the north via Vitcos, and from the east via the Inca road by Salcantay. During the 1572 colonial military expedition, the contingent that entered Vilcabamba from the south crossed the Apurimac on the only known Inca road at Osambre, well down-river to the west of Choquequirao. Balancing these factors, I believe that the neo-Inca did utilize Choquequirao at some period between 1539 and 1572, if only for cultivation and storehouses. I would agree that the ceremonial center function was abandoned, probably after the death of Huayna Capac.

3. The name Vilcabamba can be confusing. It is the name of a large mountainous region situated between the Apurimac and Urubamba Rivers westerly of Machu Picchu. The neo-Inca settlement called Vilcabamba located at Espiritu Pampa is also referred to as Vilcabamba La Vieja, to differentiate it from a later, colonial-period mining village not far from Vitcos called Vilcabamba (Vilcabamba de la Victoria de San Francisco).

4. In 1994, Lucas Cobarrubias met us at Choquequirao with the original visitors' registration book, which he claimed to have maintained since the 1920s. There were fewer than one hundred visits. Lucas said he was over a hundred years old. He lived with his wife at the site. John Hemming stayed with the family on his visit to Choquequirao in the 1960s. John tells of sleeping on a platform above the resident guinea pigs. He crossed the Apurimac River, as we did on early visits, suspended on a single cable *oroya*. A photo of the Cobarrubias family is included in his book, *The Conquest of the Incas.*

5. We had looked for years for the original Inca route to Choquequirao. We knew that a road did not come down the summit-side of the Apurimac River. During the 1990s, Cusco-based British ornithologist, Barry Walker, and I carefully explored the north side of the Apurimac drainage up to the ice fields at 14,750 feet, finding no trace of a trail. We did find an interesting site of round structures and tombs in the upper Abuela Quebrada. The routes used to access Choquequirao today are recent. The trail from Yanama through the San Juan/Victoria mines is also later.

Finally, we found it at Cotacoca. The road had long been destroyed up and down the canyon by massive floods and erosion. John

Lucus Cobarrubias and David Espejo at Choquequirao, 1994.
G. Ziegler photo.

Leivers, our determined Australian colleague, finally located the road again leading up to Pinchaunuyoc and on to Choquequirao. He found a branch leading down the lower Yanama Canyon toward the Apurimac River. Recently, John reports a trail leading downward from the llama terraces. This awaits further investigation. Do they connect?

6. In Peru, most available funding goes toward rebuilding ruins for tourist dollars, too frequently at the expense of scientific research. Unfortunately, reconstruction sometimes represents fantasy more then reality. Even the term "ruin" is no longer politically correct. "Sitio" or "complejo aqueologico" (archaeological site or complex) is the label of the moment. Some politicians seem to envision a Disneyland-esque theme park concept for Machu Picchu and other sites with tourism potential. Fortunately, Percy Paz, while subject to these political pressures, has managed to keep reconstruction at Choquequirao within reasonable bounds while undertaking excavations and studies before the evidence is forever destroyed. Percy's touch is seen in walls left uncompleted when the original could not be accurately determined.

Two

The Choquequirao Archaeological Complex and Outlying Groups

New discoveries during the last fifteen years reveal Choquequirao to be a diverse, large archaeological complex spread over more than two square miles, reaching from the depths of the river canyons below to almost the glaciers above. Several groups of well-constructed stepped terraces hang over cliffs above the Apurimac River. The finest constructions at Choquequirao are large, fitted, rectangular blocks of quartzite seen in double-jamb doorways and in corners. Walls are made of coursed, smaller blocks of mixed schist and quartzite, which were originally plastered over with tan-colored clay.

More impressive is the overall layout of the complex, incorporating the best features of Inca architecture with a genius for enhancing and emphasizing natural topography. The main structures are concentrated around two leveled plazas encompassing approximately one square mile along the crest of a rounded ridge. Inca urban design frequently incorporates two separate or distinct groups called *hurin* (lower) and *hanan* (upper). The main groups at Choquequirao appear to follow this plan.

High-Status Structures

Temples (*huacas*), important residences, and a fountain-bath system are clustered around two plazas separated by about

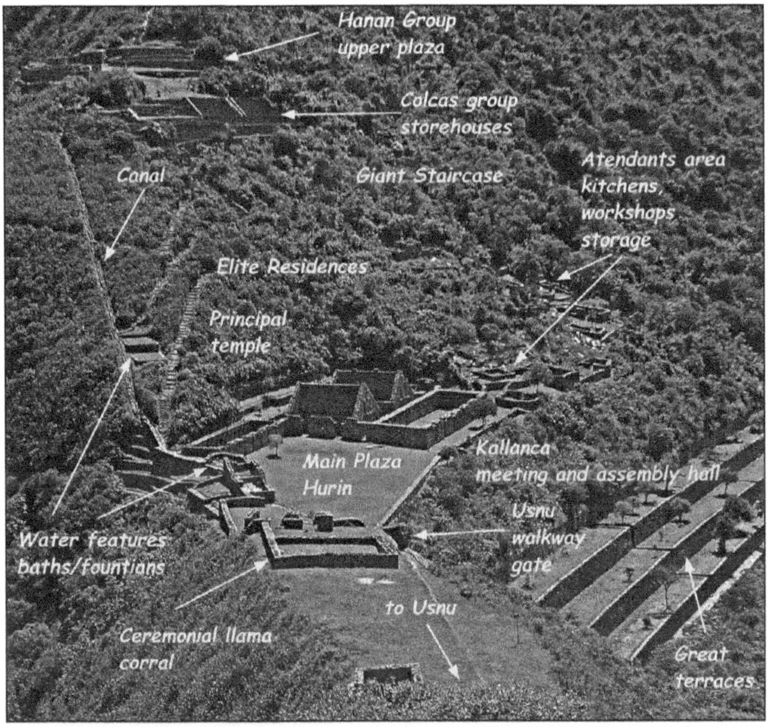

Labeled view of the main groups at Choquequirao. G. Ziegler diagram.

Water features at the Choquequirao upper plaza. Paolo Greer photo.

650 feet of elevation. The lower and larger plaza has a long multiple entrance structure that we identify as a *kallanca*—a sort of Inca multipurpose hall used for meetings, celebrations, and sometimes as a shrine.[7] A group of common buildings are clustered away from the plaza nearby. Excavations and surface items found indicate that they were probably used for workshops, food preparation, and by attendants to the residences and the *kallanca*. Between the plazas and off to the side is a group of large gabled buildings that we first identified as residences. Subsequent excavation revealed sub-floors and ventilation shafts indicating that they probably were used as storehouses for cultivated goods. Associated long, narrow structures may have been used as storage for other items, such as clothing, weapons, and tools.

Interior of the Choquequirao Principal Temple. G. Ziegler photo.

Pikiwasi—The Ridge Group

In 1996, an exploration team led by Vince Lee located a large group of structures clustered along the crest of a ridge spur running downward from the *usnu* hill. Lee cleared vegetation to survey a preliminary site plan for the group (Lee 1998). He

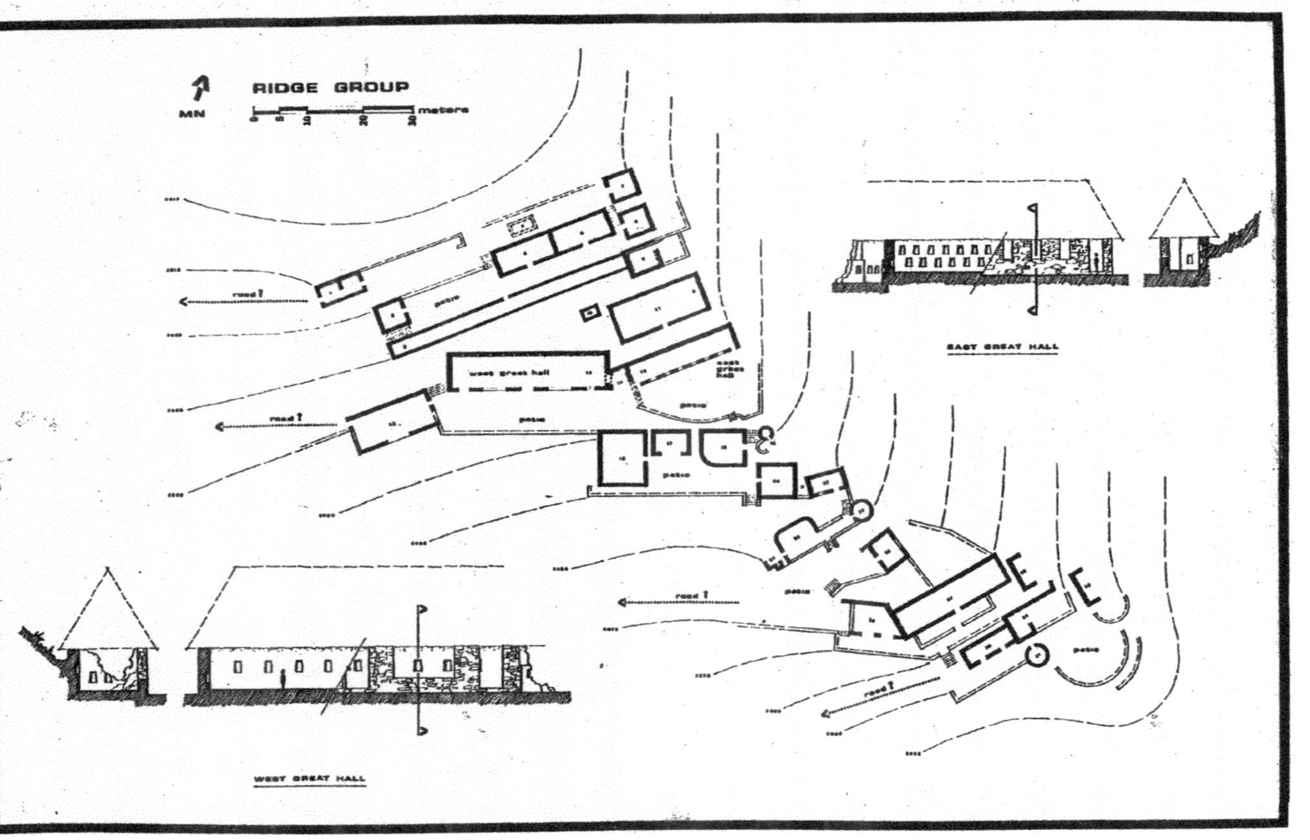

Site plan of the Ridge Group. Vince Lee diagram.

produced his usual, excellent, detailed site map. We examined the complex on several previous investigations but have learned more now that it is completely and recently cleared. The group is now named Pikiwasi by site workers, perhaps appropriately—"House of Biting Flies."

The structures and walls, as probably the rest of Choquequirao, appear to have been plastered over, inside and out, covering *pirca*-style fieldstone construction. An unusual feature is the vertically placed stone, which we and others have suggested indicates construction by imported Chachapoya workers. The buildings appear to be specialized storage structures and a large multi-door meeting hall (*kallanca*). We identified one low-walled, rectangular-shaped structure with floor-level niches as a probable guinea pig (*cuy*) nursery. No ceremonial aspects or features were identified. The complex is ideally located to catch upslope canyon breeze and abundant sun. We

Close-up of stone construction at Pikiwasi using unusual, vertically placed stone. Ken Greenwood photo.

Example of clay plastering at Choquequirao. Ken Greenwood photo.

conclude that the Ridge Group was probably designed for and functioned as a warehouse and storage area. An interesting feature is that the layout bends and blends into the contour of the ridge, a common characteristic of Inca urban design.[8]

Hurincancha

In 1999, we located another outlying group of well-made structures belonging to Choquequirao, enclosed by low walls with a stone stairway, water canal, and fountain about 1,600 feet down slope from the main groups. We named the group Hurincancha, or lower compound. Curiously, the rectangular, single-room buildings had no windows. Percy Paz suggested that they were special coca storage storehouses.[9]

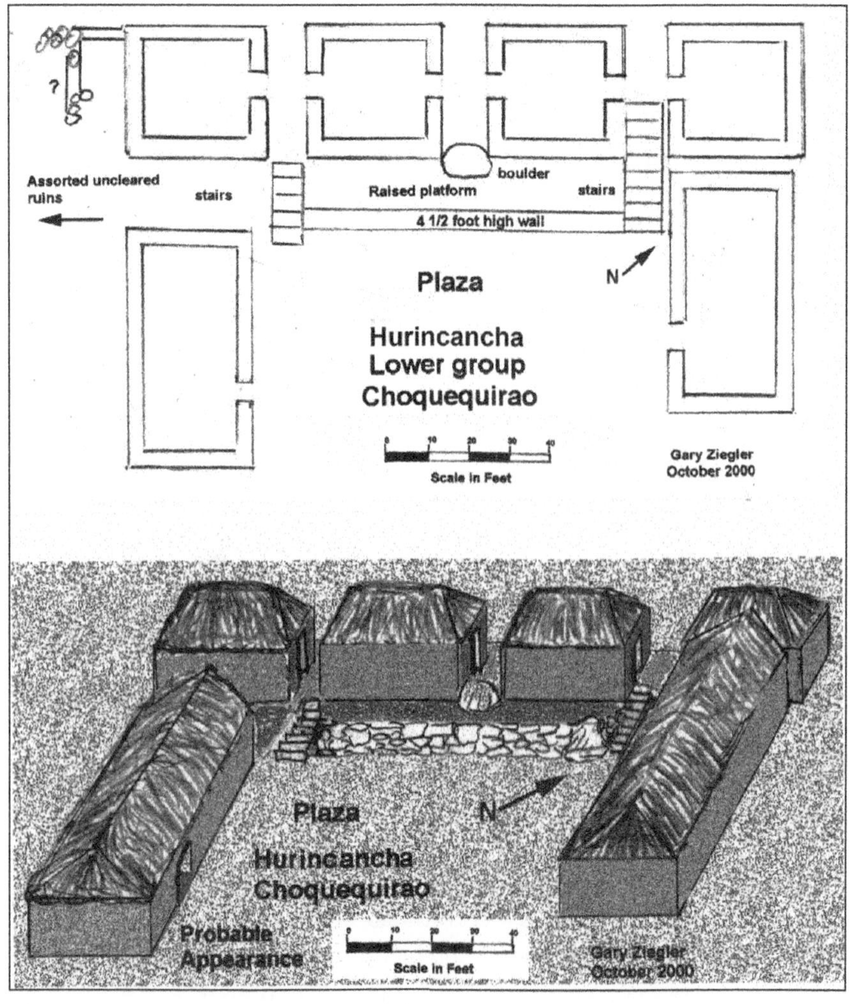

Diagram and group plan of Hurincancha. G. Ziegler diagram.

Capuliyoc

Hanging dramatically on the edge of a steep drop above the Apurimac River some distance below is a gracefully constructed group of terraces with walkways and a canal watering system positioned to receive maximum sun and warm uplift breezes from the heated canyon below. The terraces are ideally located for growing coca (Lee 1998; Paz 2004).

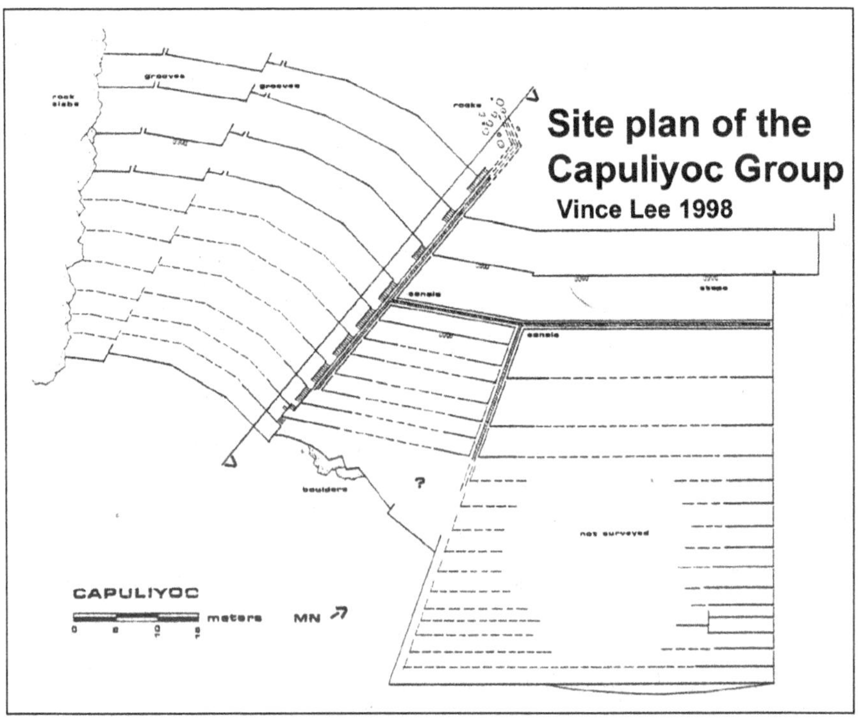

Casa de Cascada

Two unusual temple sites, incorporating carefully crafted step terraces down a steep slope, lie several hundred yards lower than the plaza groups and some distance away. Both are associated with and designed around water. The first, Casa de Cascada, or waterfall house, is located below an impressive waterfall. The other, Pinchaunuyoc, is a few miles away situated on the original Inca road leading up from Cotacoca and Yanama. In August 1998, Cusco resident author Peter Frost and Gary Ziegler examined a small group of ruins some distance below the main complex that seemed of unusual interest.

Ziegler Field Notes, 1998

We followed a recently cleared trail down to the point where the broad sloping bowl below Choquequirao drops away in cliffs. I knew of something called the waterfall house, Casa de Cascada, but was not

Image of the Casa de Cascada group and waterfall. Paolo Greer photo.

prepared for what we found. Suddenly, we are on a steeply descending stone stairway, something like the main one at Machu Picchu. Passing forty-two well-made narrow terrace walls, we arrive at three very unusual buildings, two on top of the other but offset, overlooking a deep gorge and spectacular waterfall plunging from the heights of the mountainside above. More terraces continue below. The site must be a shrine to the waterfall, which would explain its isolated location.

A canal, possibly running from a reservoir-type structure we had passed some distance above, supplied water to a nicely finished stone bath or fountain connected to the houses. We recorded the elevation as 8,005 feet, or 1,800 feet lower than the main plaza. Like many of the buildings at Choquequirao, these are unusual. The upper two houses are typically rectangular, fronting on each other with a single entranceway through a connecting wall at one side, but they differ in size.

Other buildings, such as the Outlier Group below the large platform hill and two groups, also associated with a waterfall, which we mapped at Puncuyoc near Vitcos, contain two identical houses. Here one house is larger and contains a curious L-shaped wall inside that creates a special chamber. The lower structure is L-shaped with two rooms. The top of one side connects with the base of the house above, giving it a sort of Santa Fe pueblo effect. All have numerous niches and remnants of rose-colored plaster inside and out. This complexity made for difficult diagramming. As is frequently the case, we could not get far enough away for a good photo perspective so we must rely on drawings.

What caught Peter's eye are slate cornices protruding from near the tops of several walls. These are selectively installed over the entrance doorway walls on all three structures. The COPESCO crew believes that they were placed to protect the plaster, but I disagree, as they are only on certain walls. I think that they were decoratively incorporated into the design and had no practical function. Other slates are found in abundance at the main groups above, but none remain in place to determine original placement. The only places that we have seen similar cornices are Chachapoya sites in northern Peru. Did Chachapoya workers leave a part of their home style here?"

Peruvian Architect Roberto Samanez and archaeologist Julio Zapata, who conducted the original study of Choquequirao for the COPESCO project in 1986, write that the waterfall group functioned as a ceremonial feature associated with water flowing down the Quebrada Chunchumayo from glacial melt of the sacred mountain, or *apu*, above. A circular route from

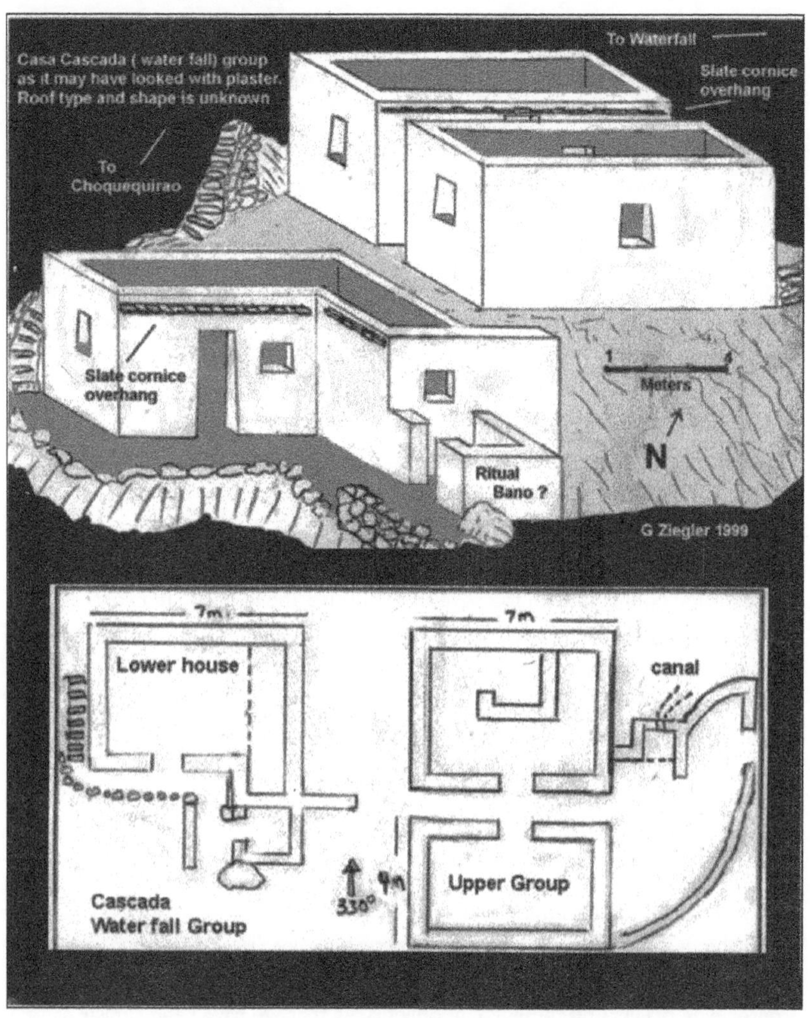

the main plaza groups represents a ritual pathway for seasonal ceremonies to and from the waterfall structures. They theorize that the group served as a ritual retreat and residence for the provincial Inca governor in charge of Choquequirao during colder months (Samanez and Zapata 2003).

Pinchaunuyoc

Pinchaunuyoc (place of the spring) is a very special shrine associated with the only significant flowing water on an otherwise dry mountainside. A small exploratory expedition led by Hugh Thomson first reported the site in 1982. Barry Walker (see Acknowledgments) and a group of Cusco-based adventurers called "The Ramblers," visited it again in 1984. Barry was with us later when we re-opened the old trail there in 1994 during a documentary filming expedition.

Cleared terraces at Pinchaunuyoc. Hugh Thomson photo.

Pinchaunuyoc consists of a number of narrow, walled terraces aligned with and complimenting the contours of a steep, incised arroyo, a graceful effect that is achieved by inclining carefully made walls some 25 degrees and achieving a curving effect by a setback or zig-zag of each wall at intervals. The walls are about 8 feet high at the center of the site but taper down in height as they curve outward. Constructed from native metamorphic rock, which fractures along parallel flat surfaces, flat edges are aligned to face outward giving a pleasing smooth surface to the wall.

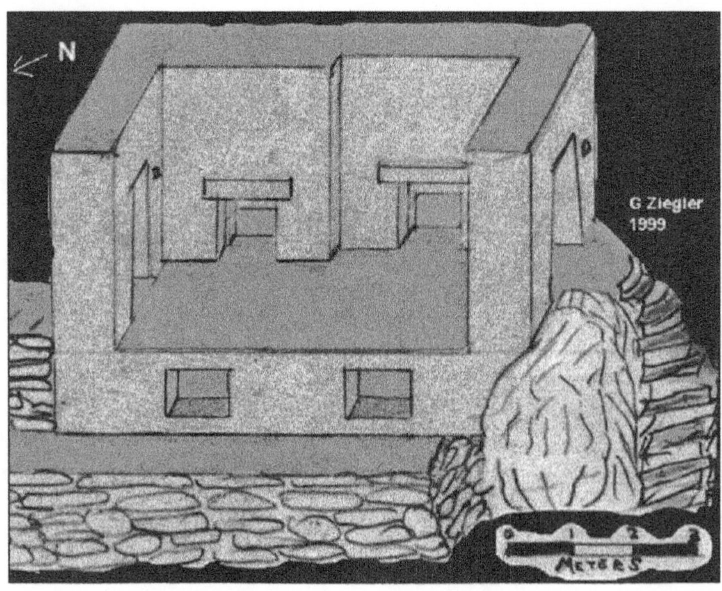

Drawing of the main shrine at Pinchaunuyoc. G. Ziegler diagram.

Unique to this site is vertically coursed stonework with a flat cap rock placed horizontally on top. Corners are made with worked stones. Typically, many large boulders are incorporated within the coursed masonry. The standard three offset step-stones set at regular intervals seen in many Inca terrace walls are present, but seem more decorative than functional.

Two unique buildings, which we call shrines (*huacas*), a gracefully curving stairway, and a system of stone baths or fountains dominate the central and largest terraces. Remarkably, water is still flowing through these basins centered between the buildings. Both structures are constructed with normal horizontally coursed stone, fitted with mortar, and plastered over with a fine clay covering. Enough of the plaster remains to see that it was colored something between rose and orange.

The larger of the two building, measuring 18x11.5 feet inside, has double-jamb doorways and inside recessed niches usually reserved for important structures. These however, are almost rectangular, unusual for the trapezoidal-minded Inca.

Double-jamb entrance at Pinchaunuyoc. Lillian Roberts photo.

The front of the building is left open, undoubtedly for the view and associated ritual. The structure faces the June solstice sunset at 293 degrees (magnetic) and is located in the center of the semi-circular terraces. The imposing, pointed summit of Cerro Victoria, with a sacred platform, *usnu*, and tombs on top, lies directly on a north azimuth from the structure. As we have learned from previous studies, this probably is not a coincidence.

The smaller structure is similarly constructed, but is a curious multi-angled affair with several offset internal walls with multiple niches, like several other buildings at Choquequirao. This unusual group of well-made terraces, multi-angled shrines and a flowing water system of fountains, baths, and canals was completely cleared and reconstructed several years ago. Unlike some other such re-constructions, this was carefully and accurately done, probably under the guidance of Percy Paz. In comparison with photos, diagrams, and drawings made when we originally partially cleared and studied the site in 1995, nothing seems enhanced or fantasized. The structures have appropriately been only structurally reinforced and some partially crumbled walls set back in place.

Pinchaunuyoc is seemingly in the middle of nowhere. In actuality, it was the spiritually symbolic main entrance portal to Choquequirao. During the 2002 Cotacoca exploration, we learned that the continuation of the Inca road down the Yanama Valley did not go back up and over San Juan Pass, the present route, but instead passed through the site complex of Cotacoca along the river below. Crossing the tributary Rio Blanco, the route then climbed through Pinchaunuyoc's multiple terraces, fountains, and shrine structures to continue up and over the mountain above to reach the main complex at Choquequirao.

View toward the Yanama Valley and Cotacoca.
Lillian Roberts photo.

The Inca road enters a stepped walkway leading up to the water features, then passes along a terrace below the principal central shrine. This first spiritually important contact with Choquequirao is passage through a *huaca* site, which we believe was dedicated to the flowing spring, the one water source on the mountainside. The analogy is similar to the water sites of Winay Wayna and Sector II of Llactapata located on the separate approaches to Machu Picchu. We believe these may represent special *huacas* associated with a pilgrimage route and sacred walkway.

Above Pinchaunuyoc, the hillside contains hundreds of round, low, fieldstone walls and open fields suitable for growing maize and other food products. Flat grinding stones are strewn about. We suggest that the wall remains represent the base or retaining walls for houses that were made from wood. This large settlement and cultivatable hillside would have housed workers and a sizable resident population in support of Choquequirao.[10]

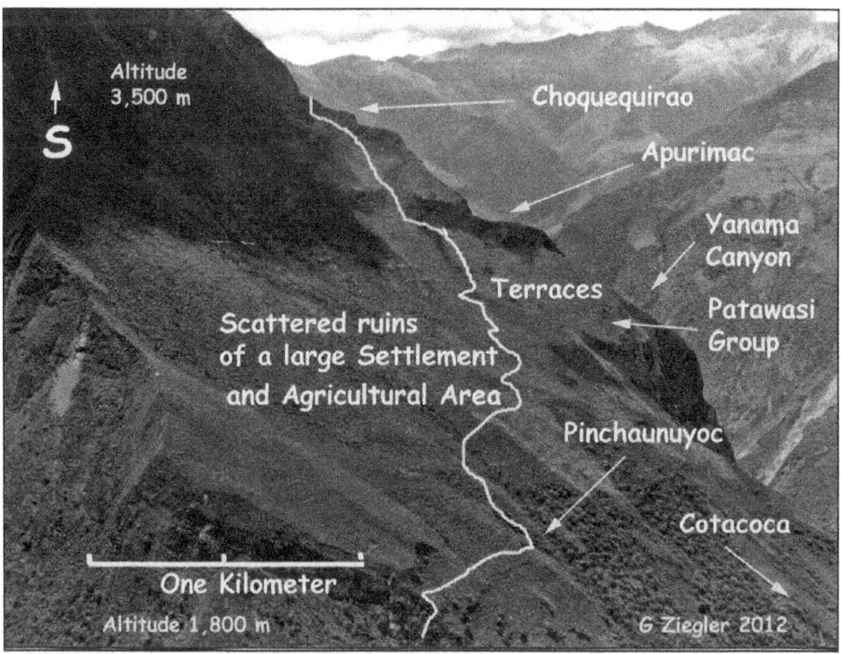

View of the Pinchaunuyoc hillside and route to Choquequirao. G. Ziegler diagram.

The Usnu

Rising imposingly above the Lower Plaza at Pinchaunuyoc is a large artificially truncated hill—an *usnu*, or sacred platform. The path to the hill passes through a well-made double-

Diagram of the Choquequirao Lower Plaza group at Pinchaunuyoc looking south toward the *usnu* hill. G. Ziegler diagram.

jamb entrance attached to an unusual, complex temple structure with tall niches, hidden passages, and multiple entrances. Behind and above the entrance and temple are low-walled enclosures, corrals which we suggest may have been used to contain llamas for sacrificial ceremonies (Paz 2004). The top of the *usnu* has been leveled and ringed by low retaining walls, forming a 54-yard wide, oval-shaped platform. The view is impressive—the deep Apurimac Canyon meanders below. Five glacier-covered peaks, canyons, summits, and ridges dominate the surrounding horizon (Ziegler 1999). Two similar *usnu* platforms can be seen to the north above the Yanama Canyon on Cerro Victoria at the Inca site called Corihuayrachina. Vince Lee has recently traced a line of sites from platform to platform onward to Machu Picchu.[11] (Ziegler 2001).

Like Huayna Picchu, which lies directly north of Machu Picchu's Sacred Plaza, the *usnu* hill lies directly south of Choquequirao's main monumental groups centered on the ridge saddle and continuing up the raising slope behind. The central axis of both royal estates is north-south. Again, we don't believe this to be coincidental. We conclude that Choquequirao was modeled after Machu Picchu.

Casa de Sacerdotes

Image of the Sacerdotes group. Lillian Roberts photo.

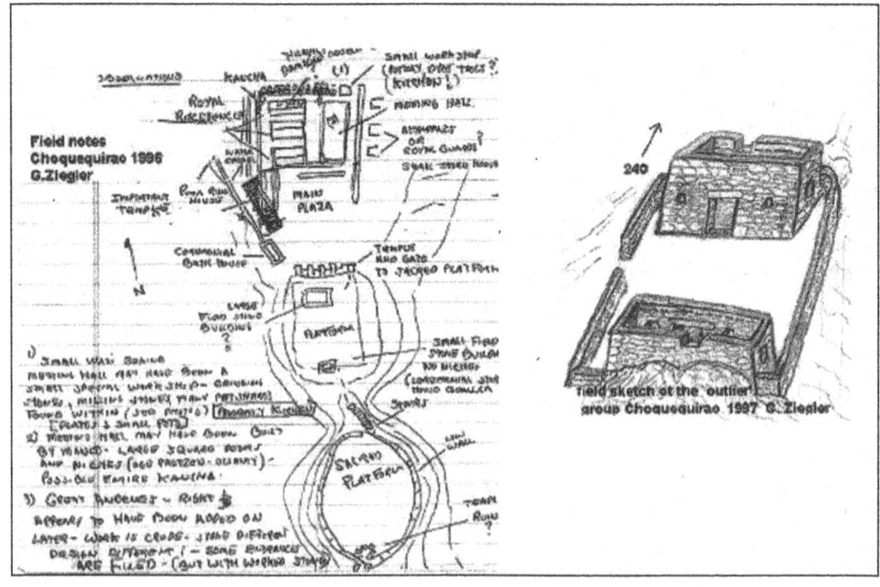

Sketch and field notes of Casa de Sacerdotes at Choquequirao. G. Ziegler diagram.

A walkway from the *usnu* descends the opposite side a 160 yards or so to arrive at another small, high-walled enclosure that Bingham called the Outlier Group (Bingham 1910), now named Casa de Sacerdotes. This group, a small compound aligned on a ridge saddle like those at Machu Picchu, Pisac, and the main groups of Choquequirao, contains two identical single-room structures facing each other. Percy Paz, Choquequirao's expert and definitive authority, believed they housed the high priest staff in a spiritually charged setting. This seems a likely interpretation.

Llamayoc—Place of the Llamas

An important more recent discovery is the uncovering of the extensive stepped-stone terraces of Llamayoc, inlaid with white quartzite figures representing a caravan of 22 cargo-laden llamas and their human handler. The uppermost wall has a white inlaid zig-zag pattern. Some 130 well-made stepped terraces gracefully contour down the steep ridge side below the main plaza, facing and focusing on the deep Apurimac gorge

Image of the upper wall at Llamayoc. G. Ziegler photo.

View of the llama terraces at Llamayoc. Hugh Thomson photo.

Llama figures made from white quartzite. G. Ziegler photo.

below, the June solstice setting, and the ice peak Panta. A small stone-lined fountain or bath is placed close to a walkway near the lower terraces. The llamas face left from the viewer in the direction of the village of Yanama and the high peaks of Corihuayrachina, Viracochan, Choqueticarpo, and Pumasillo.

Percy Paz convincingly argues that Choquequirao was a major cultivation and distribution center of coca during imperial times. Llama trains carried the coca down from Choquequirao, passing through the water shrine of Pinchaunuyoc to the Yanama River Canyon and Cotacoca, then on to Cusco and the empire on well-made, maintained roads, called Inca nan.

Large pastoral areas and the remains of immense stone corral enclosures can be seen on the high *puna* (timberline) near the Inca road toward Mollepata and Machu Picchu (Paz 2004). During the exploration of Cotacoca in 2002, we diagramed similar large enclosures there that we identified as llama corrals. Llamas have a long history in the Andes as carriers of cargo and as ceremonial entities (D'Altroy 2003; Paz 1988). Percy suggested that the llama figures incorporated in the terrace walls along with smaller holding enclosures on the walkway to the *usnu* platform strongly indicate a llama ceremonial focus at Choquequirao (Paz 2004).

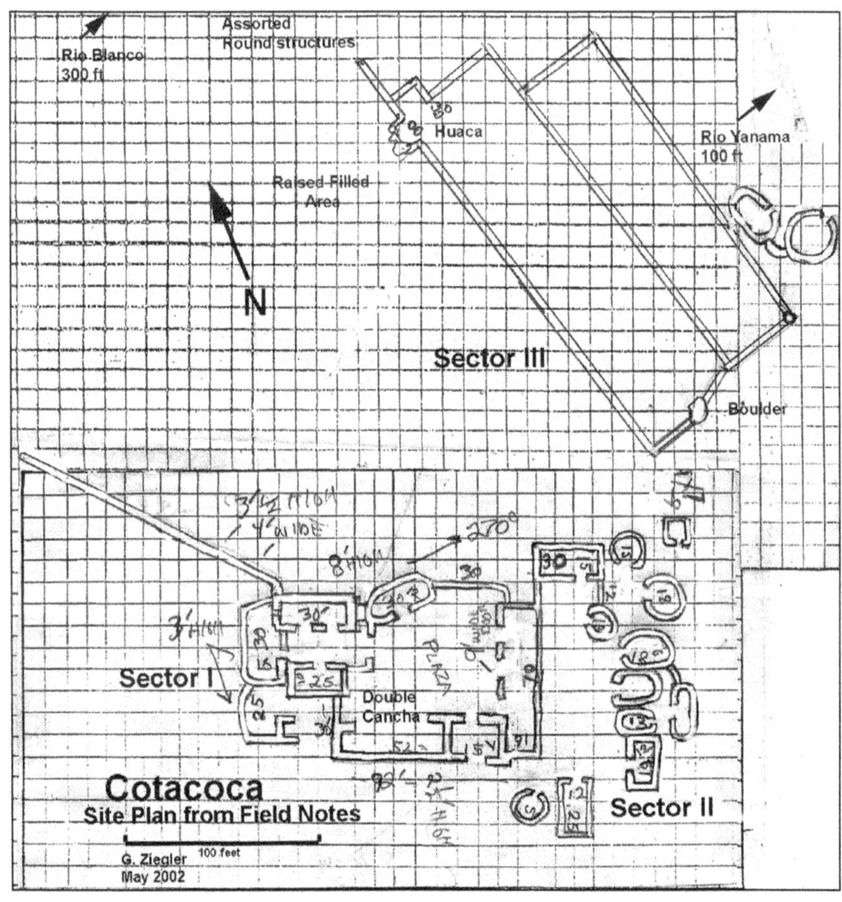

View of Yanama
River and Cotacoca
from Pinchaunuyoc.
Paolo Greer photo.

View of the
Apurimac River
from Llamayoc.
G. Ziegler photo.

Notes

7. Tom Zuidema told us about a large *kallanca* on the approach to Cusco that had been a sort of shrine, with offering required from those passing by.

8. Ziegler Field Notes, 1998

We took a good look at Vince Lee's "Ridge Group." He did a remarkable job getting this mapped out, considering the density of foliage and difficulty in moving around. We found a few differences and some compass deviation, but all in all, the mapping is good. I have not had time to ponder where this group fits in the big *choque* [summit] picture. They will need a lot more study and examination. My first impression is that this area was lower-status and primarily functional. I saw only one structure that I would call ceremonial. The rest seem to be built for housing, meetings, etc. Several tall windowless structures may have been for storage. Most windows, niches, and doorways were rectangular or square. I did not see any interior wall or corner pegs, as are common with the main plaza group.

The group layout is curious, with several buildings out of sync with the majority but lining up with others located at a different level. The general flow of structures, walls, and terraces is typically in harmony with the flow of the ridge line and quite nice. I considered the possibility that the group may have dated from a later time, but have no real evidence except similar construction. It will be interesting to see what the archaeological record reveals when the crew cleans it up.

9. Percy Paz, personal communication
Ziegler Field Notes, 1999

With GPS in hand we attempt to locate the group of houses that our party had stumbled upon last year. We have been together for some time having completed the long trek from Huancacalle. All are eager to help with clearing and mapping this new find.

After the usual thrashing about in the thorny thickets that make up much of the vegetation on the mountainside below the Great Andenes, we arrive at the place indicated by the GPS that I had logged in last year for the site. Zip … nothing here. Mystified, we disperse outward in a circle looking for evidence of walls. An hour or so later and several hundred feet away, we find our objective, a hidden plaza enclosed by covered remains of crumbling buildings tucked away in a grove on the mountain.

I have used a GPS for a number of years and have always been able to accurately return to marked way points, a testimony to why I probably have not run aground on recent annual sailing trips. I read that the U.S. has re-calibrated its navigational satellites to remove a programmed error factor. Ah so … my readings last year reflect an error significant enough that we could not immediately locate the marked position. Anyway, here we are with plenty of time. We use up the remaining daylight clearing and measuring the site.

The group is a nicely laid out *cancha* [compound of houses enclosed by a wall], slightly non-symmetrical, open toward the Apurimac. Curiously, we find no niches or windows. I am thinking storehouses but the layout around a plaza, nice stairways, etc. would make them unusual. Another idea I keep trying to justify is that a road must have come up this side from the Apurimac. If so, this could have been the *tambo* [control station] on the final approach to the main groups above. Amy Finger found what she thinks is the ruin of a gateway below. As I recall, the Ridge Group has one as well? Or more likely, the site (we name it Hurincancha, meaning lower group) was probably an outlying residence, perhaps, or the caretakers of Capuliyoc some distance below, but why no windows …?

10. Ziegler Field Notes, 1999

We were able to more thoroughly investigate this extensive area—thanks to a recent fire of unknown origin, we discover that the entire mountainside above the site is now clear. This area has been a major focus for ongoing exploration but due to the tangle of brush and tough bamboo, we were only able to explore small portions each year with great effort. Finally, in one long day we are able to completely examine the entire square mile area. We humorously labeled it pyro-archaeology.

From Pinchaunuyoc upward to steep cliffs 3,000 feet above, the slope is covered with agricultural terraces and the remains of crude retainer walls. A number of large corn grinding stones are lying about, giving a good indication of what the principal crop was. Previously, we had located many groups of low round foundations. We studied one group of more than twenty-four structures stretching vertically along a small rounded ridge. These measure 18 feet in diameter and generally 3 feet high and are well made with horizontally coursed, thin 2-inch thick stones. The structures sit upon flat earthen platforms formed by equally well-made half-circle retaining walls at differing levels up the gentle slope.

At first I thought the circles were foundations or remains of higher walls, as some are set into the hillside and are higher. On closer observation, we realized that the walls were actually intact and were the original height. Fallen walls would have left piles of stones. Then we found a large flat grinding stone in the center of one of the circles, apparently sitting where it had been abandoned. Suddenly, I realized that we were looking at the floor of a round wood or bamboo house, which had once been inside the stone ring. This makes sense, as an immense farming area requires a large settlement of lower-status workers.

Building stones and walls above Pinchaunuyoc.
Amy Finger photo.

11. Vince Lee, personal communication. He believes that these distant, line-of-sight platforms were built as part of a rapid communication system to Cusco and points in between utilizing signal fires, something like modern day texting—a few words or a couple of fires will get the message conveyed.

Three
Architectural Features and Construction at Choquequirao

View of the Hurin Temple from the Lower Plaza. G. Ziegler photo.

Inca construction at Choquequirao is unique in several ways. Unlike Cusco, where fine polygonal and coursed-walls are made of limestone and andesite, or at Machu Picchu where monumental features are carefully sculptured from granite, the fragile in-situ metamorphic rock available at Choquequirao cannot be so shaped.[12] The builders were forced to create a different style of monumental construction. Entrances and corners were shaped from rounded quartzite, but the rough coursed-ashlar walls were clay-plastered over inside and out, then painted rose or a light orange color (discussed more in Chapter Eight). Unappreciative of the geological restrictions, Bingham and others discounted Choquequirao as lacking in high-status architectural quality and thereby importance when compared to Machu Picchu and Cusco (Ziegler 1999).

We know from many sources that the Inca deployed labor and specialists (*Mitimae*) imported from around the empire. A traditional Andean communal group (*ayllu*) named Chachapoya was reported at Cachora, across the Apurimac from Choquequirao in 1689 (Villanueva 1982). Chachapoyans were reportedly resettled in the Yucay Valley north of Cusco (Cieza 1967; D'Altroy 2003).[13]

Double jamb entrance and vertically aligned stones at Pinchaunuyoc

Thomson 2010-

During early visits to Choquequirao, we noticed unusual vertically aligned masonry. The waterfall shrine, Casa de Cascada, exhibits uncharacteristic slate cornices protruding from walls resembling a style seen at Chachapoya sites in northern

Peru. The walls with the llama figures and a zig-zag inlaid pattern are uniquely Chachapoya style, not seen elsewhere in Inca construction.[14] (Paz 2004). It seems certain that laborers and specialists from Chachapoya helped build Choquequirao. It may be one of the few Inca sites where an imported ethnic labor group can be identified as an almost certainty.

Machu Picchu has storehouses, workshops, higher- and lower-status living quarters, and multiple temples that probably supported different calendar scheduled activities. However, the predominance of features and the overall design suggests mountain and sun worship as the primary focus and ritual activity (Ziegler and Malville 2006). Choquequirao appears similar in ritual focus. The archaeological evidence indicates that both estates were undergoing continuing construction and modifications until abandonment. It is likely that usage and activities changed when administration shifted to a royal Inca lineage group (*panaca*) following the death of the founding Inca.

Machu Picchu was abandoned before or during the arrival of the Spanish at Cusco in 1533, probably having fallen into isolation and disuse during the civil wars and concurrent epidemics (Ziegler and Malville 2006). Choquequirao may have been abandoned at the same time then reoccupied for an unknown period after 1533 or during the neo-Inca resistance of 1536–72. Based upon reference to an *encomienda*, a colonial land grant held by Hernando Pizarro containing a place called Chuquicarando, Erwan Duffait suggests that this was likely Choquequirao. He reasons that if so, Choquequirao would have been occupied after 1572. However, no archeological evidence has been found to support this (Duffait 2005).

Activities at Choquequirao would have been greatly modified if occupied by the last Incas. Several stairway corridors are filled in and blocked on the giant terraces. A number of windows and entrances are blocked at the storehouse (*colca*) sector. Frequently, Andean archaeological sites have been adapted in later times by local herders and farmers as convenient walled

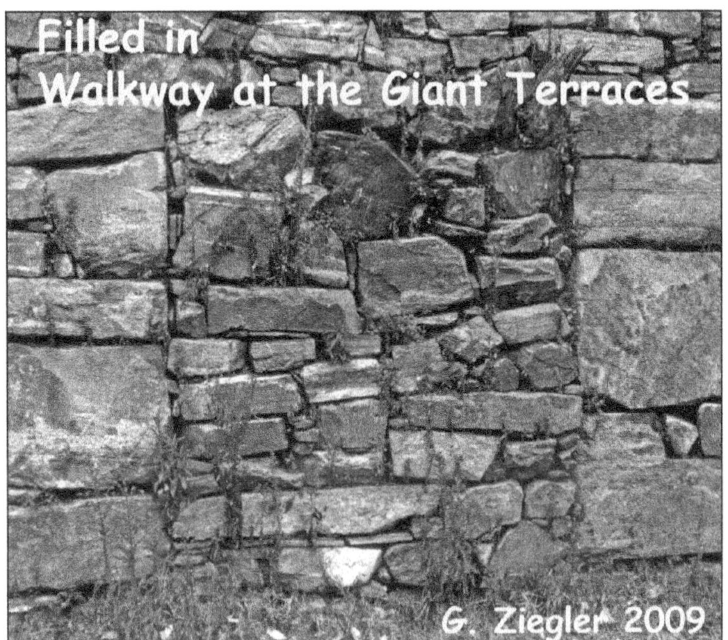

Filled in passage at Choquequirao. G. Ziegler photo.

G. Ziegler at the Upper Temple group at Choquequirao.
Paolo Greer photo.

gardens, corrals for cattle, and ready residences. This does not seem the case at Choquequirao. Generally, colonial or later-period modifications consist of crude fieldstone filling. The modifications at Choquequirao were constructed more carefully with fitted stones to almost resemble the original Inca masonry. This may represent an attempt to make the sectors more defensible after the last Inca return in 1537, or perhaps only an insignificant modification perpetuated by one of Topa Inca's *panaca* caretakers. It will remain an enigma.

If Choquequirao was Topa Inca's favorite estate, it is probable that his *panaca* would have maintained a shrine or mausoleum containing Topa's *huaque* (mummy replicas) representative. We have no evidence for this, but if so, the curious multi-roomed building at the upper plaza would have been the likely place. This group with its small, irregular plaza incorporates two interesting features along with several plain, rectangular-shaped structures. The first is a well-made bath or fountain enclosed by a low wall. This begins a manipulated water flow system that feeds the Lower Plaza groups and is then diverted on to the ridge group of Pikiwasi and Llamayoc, some distance below the ridge crest.

The second interesting feature is a curious, single-story shrine-like structure with multiple internal angles and double niches. We speculate that sacred objects, perhaps mummy replicas (*huaques*) were placed there during special ceremonial events, or more wildly speculating, it was the estate builder Topa Inca's mausoleum permanently housing his mummy replica, maintained by *panaca* attendants. The building, connected wall, and water feature face south toward the *usnu* hill and the distant ice peak, Apu Ampay. There seems to be no solstice alignment.

Notes

12. The underlying structural rock for much of the region west of Machu Picchu consists of older sedimentary material altered by heat and pressure, metamorphosed into mica schist and ancient sand-

stones compressed into quartzite. Reflecting parallel alignment of formative bedding planes, the fragile schist resists being shaped into anything but flat pieces, which must have frustrated Inca builders. It is impossible to shape polygonal structural stones from schist. The somewhat more formable quartzite was used for cornerstones and doorways. Igneous basalt was imported for roof, wall pegs, and eye bonder stones.

13. Our Andean Research Project exploration in 2007 investigated undocumented sites on the east side of the Urubamba River between Machu Picchu and Chaullay. A number consisted of round structures with features characteristic of Chachapoya construction. We also looked at a site called Inca Carcel reported by Robert Von Kaupp to be Chachapoya (Von Kaupp and Fernandez 2010).

14. In 1997, Frank Ciampa, a veteran of the Gene Savoy expeditions, Peter Frost, David Espejo, and I put together an expedition to Chachapoyas specifically to compare features there with what we had observed at Choquequirao. We visited Gene Savoy's Gran Vilaya complex and documented a new group we humorously named "Chacha Picchu."

G. Ziegler photo.

Savoy was a legendary explorer and eccentric self-promoter, founder of his own Reno, Nevada, church and authentic discoverer of the real "Lost City of the Incas"—Vilcabamba at Espiritu

Pampa. He had a sort of cult following of attractive and wealthy women. His modus operandi was to find a site, or several loosely associated groups, then claim it was part of a huge complex encompassing many square miles. If something later was found by someone else, it was only a part of his Grand something or other.

While I was studying at San Marcos, the national university in Lima, the news was full of Savoy's discoveries at Espiritu Pampa. Sponsored by the Patronata de Arqueologia, predecessor to the INC (Instituto Nacional de Cultura) and the Newspaper, *El Comercio*, Jorge Moreau, journalist and head photographer from the paper and I organized a group to check out his reports. Some suspected that he was looting the site, so our job was to gather the truth. As these were the years of the violent Hugo Blanco insurgency, we traveled well armed with a contingent of national police and army mules. Struggling through deep mud and pouring rains of the rainy season in January 1965, we arrived to verify Savoy's work as legitimate. Many years later, I conveyed this story to Savoy who humorously told me that he was hiding at the village of Lucma, watching us with binoculars as we rode past, wondering who the pistol-toting Gringo was. He expected to be arrested if found, which of course he would have been.

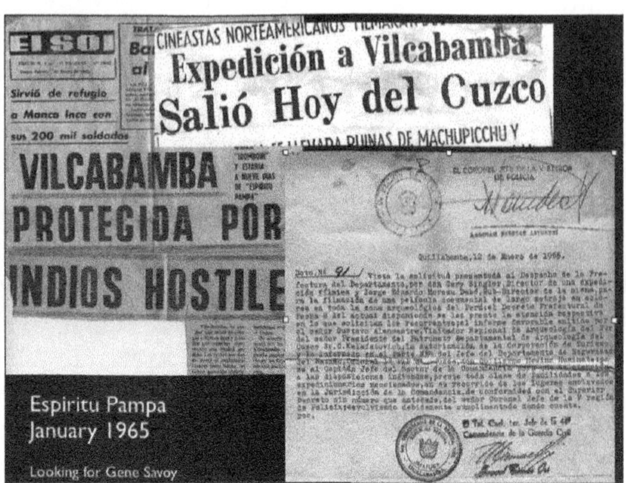
El Sol
Sirvió de refugio a Manco Inca con sus 200 mil soldados
VILCABAMBA PROTEGIDA POR INDIOS HOSTILE
CINEASTAS NORTEAMERICANOS
Expedición a Vilcabamba Salió Hoy del Cuzco
RUINAS DE MACHUPICCHU Y

News headlines and government letter of authorization for the 1965 Espiritu Pampa expedition. G. Ziegler diagram

Journalist Jorge Moreau and police on the trail to Espiritu Pampa.
G. Ziegler photo.

We finally met for the first time in Lima following our return from Chachapoyas. Frank, Gill Hazel, and I were invited to his apartments in Miraflores for the evening. He greeted us dressed in an oversized, white frilled shirt, wearing a large jeweled medallion with ancient-looking symbols inscribed on ponderous gold. At his arm was his "research assistant" and a kind of high priestess in his church. She poured us a round of single malts while setting out a silver, also jeweled, cigarette case for the table. Producing a long, dark, ebony cigarette holder, she put it to her lips, lit a cigarette with a vintage Ronson, artful exhaled, then passed it to Gene to smoke while we talked. It was a most interesting, unforgettable evening. We made the most of it. Gill, a good-humored Australian gal who really did help with research, coined a phrase for herself modeled after the Savoy show—"archaeo-bimbo."

Four
Andean Astronomy and the Sacred Landscape

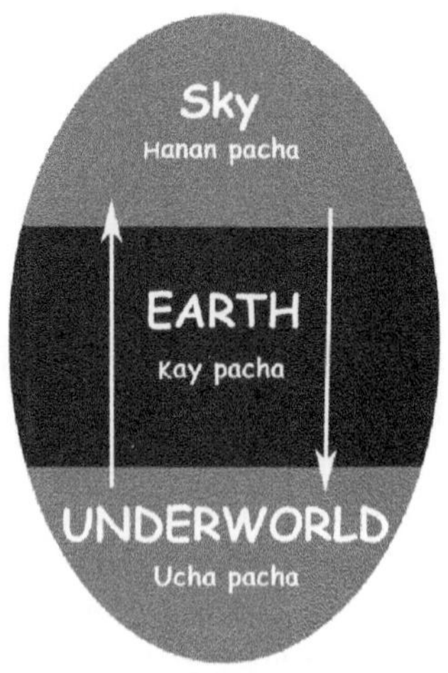

The Andean Cosmos: Movement between the worlds was symbolized by stairs, underground labyrinths, caves, *huacas,* and *usnus.*

The cosmos of the Incas consisted of three distinct worlds—that of *Ucha Pacha,* the underworld; *Kay Pacha,* the here and now; and *Hanan Pacha,* the world above (Urton 1981). Each world was represented by a sacred animal: *Hanan Pacha* by the condor, *Kay Pacha* the puma, and *Ucha Pacha* the serpent, and stone carvings of these creatures are common. The Inca apparently believed that rock could be empowered and energized through elaborate carving (Niles 1999). Pachacuti apparently believed that he could improve upon the natural world and, as the son of the sun and co-creator of the land, he could modify and enhance the work of the creator.

Many of these improvements to rocks seem to have been state-controlled and likely guided by tradition and an established artisan's class. The sculpted rock *huacas* of Cusco and the Sacred Valley do not suggest graffiti-like innovation, but rather symbolism and meaning developed over considerable time by Andean cultures (Niles 1999; Paternosto 1989).

Embedded in the earth, these sculpted manifestations of the sacred were connected with the powers of the underworld and became venerated, once they were enhanced through elaborate carving. Sculpted outcroppings, as *huacas,* were an important part of cosmological symbolism regarding the three worlds of the Inca (Paternosto 1989). The Inca also used carved rocks as a vehicle to promote state ideology and the solar religion. They were symbols of commemoration, mediation with the cosmos, and state identity, all the while remaining part of their perception of their sacred relationship with nature and the land (Van deGutche 1990).

Channeled water feature at Quillarumiyoc. Catherine McGuire photo.

Running water was understood to be an energizing and animating life force in Andean cultures, known in Quechua as "*camay.*" In the cosmology described in the Huarochirí manuscript, life is born from the embrace of feminine earth by masculine water, homologous to the growth of plants from soil when moistened by water (Salomon and Urioste 1991). The circulation of running water and the pouring of offertory liquids could animate certain inanimate objects to become sentient beings with extraordinary and superhuman powers (D'Altroy 2003; Salomon and Urioste 1991).

Water empowered *huacas* through a life-energizing force

that could be used to provide sentience to the inanimate or renew power in the living (Salomon and Urioste, 1991).

The world's water cycled through the heavens and earth in its journey down the Vilcanota River with return via the Milky Way (Urton 1981). Inca cosmology viewed the Milky Way as a river flowing across the night sky in a very literal sense. They saw earthly waters as being drawn into the heavens and then later returned to earth following a celestial rejuvenation. The earth was thought to float in a cosmic ocean (Urton 1981). When the celestial river's orientation was such that it dipped into that ocean, waters were then drawn into the sky. "The Milky Way is therefore an integral part of the continuing recycling of water throughout the Quechua universe" (Urton 1981:60).

Huacas and Usnus

Sculptured stone head at Chavín de Huantar. Kim Malville photo.

Andean cosmology has deep roots extending back at least to Caral, an early pre-ceramic, coastal center dating to 2600 BCE, where processional stairways connect the underworld represented by a lower circular plaza to the upper world at the summit of the Great Pyramid. At Chavín de Huantar, 1500–300 BCE, cosmological ceremonies are revealed by uniquely Andean artifacts: *huacas* (Bray 2009; Gullberg 2010; Malville et al. 2009) and *usnus,* which are raised ceremonial platforms sometimes with basins or wells into which offerings were poured. The carved 15-foot tall shaft of the Lanzón of Chavín is a well-known example of an early *huaca*, an evocative axis *mundi*, linking the three worlds of sky, earth, and the underworld (Burger 1992). Although it thrusts upward toward the sky, it is set deep in the interior of the Old Temple, reached by labyrinthine passageways. It is carved with the image of the supreme deity of Chavín, a fierce transformation of a shaman priest into a fanged jaguar with swirling snakes.

Replication of the horizon at Yuroc Rumi. G. Ziegler diagram.

Huacas continued to be central elements in Andean cosmology for at least another two thousand years, continuing a tradition of penetrating the three worlds through their verticality and shamanic-like power of transformation (Burger 1992; Eliade 1964; Staller 2008). *Huacas* possessed supernatural power and an animating essence for people, crops, and animals (Malville 2009; Staller 2008).

One of the roles of Andean religion and ritual was to keep the universe in balance and harmony, such that water was abundant and crops would flourish. Some of the ritual offerings to *huacas* were water, corn beer (*chicha*), and blood, which were poured into basins or channels as a form of sympathetic magic to stimulate the flow of energy through the cosmos.

Shamanic transcendence through the three planes of the cosmos was a continuing theme in Andean cosmology. Symbolic stairways linking the dark underworld of caves and labyrinths to the earth and sky are ubiquitous, such as at Chavín, Chankillo, Chinchero, and Machu Picchu.

View of Chankillo. Carlos Aranibar photo.

Chankillo, in the Casma-Sechín river basin, followed the collapse of the Chavín civilization and was occupied between 320–200 BCE (Ghezzi 2011). With its hilltop fort, cloistered temple, thirteen towers, and extensive structures, Chankillo seems to be a complex mixture of warfare and ceremony.

The major axis of Chankillo is solar, extending from December solstice sunrise to June solstice sunset. There also is evidence for interest in major lunar standstills. Ghezzi (2011) presents a convincing argument that the great fortress may have been a scene of ritual battles. Others have suggested a similar interpretation for nearby Cerro Sechín, such that mythical battles were performed as a form of ritual dance.

The towers of Chankillo may have been the scene of ritual processions. Each of the thirteen towers has double stairways, suggesting that they were *huacas* and that shamanic movement between the worlds was their raison d'être. Furthermore, the orientation of each tower is gradually changed from terrestrial to solar as one ascends to the sky (Malville et al. 2009).

The interactive parallelism of the three worlds is another feature of Andean cosmology. The Milky Way was understood to be the celestial counterpart of the Urubamba River (Urton 1981) and dark sky constellations such as the Celestial Llama provided the life force for terrestrial llamas (Bauer and Dearborn 1995; Salomon and Urioste 1991).

The Spanish were immensely puzzled by *huacas*. For them *huacas* were very alien features in an already alien land. As documented by the chroniclers, *huacas* were carved and uncarved rocks, idols, buildings, springs, caves, poles, trees, nails, hair and body parts of Incas, mummies of ancestors, children born with deformities, piles of stones on mountain passes, and places where lightning had struck (Van deGutche 1990).

Archaeologist Tamara Bray (2009) is a major advocate for the emerging paradigm in anthropology that uses the ethnohistoric record to explore alternate Andean ontologies (branch of metaphysics dealing with the nature of being). In particular, she recommends that to understand the Andean world, we need to break out of Cartesian dualism in which living and non-living are fundamentally different. Applied to the astronomy of the Inca, this "different understanding of the nature and categories of being on the part of indigenous people in the Andes" implies that we should free ourselves of the notion that the stones of Cusco or Machu Picchu were inert lumps of inanimate matter, the sole meaning and function of which was to mark astronomical sightlines (Bray 2009:357).

The ethnography of *huacas* indicates that they were regarded as living beings possessing extraordinary powers and the great wisdom of ancestors (Bray 2009; D'Altroy 2003; Salomon and Urioste 1991). They had vibrant lives functioning as oracles and dispensing wisdom; they were fed and dressed in clothes; they could be married, abducted, or even destroyed by enemies. The personhood of *huacas* blurs the distinctions between the living and the dead, between animate and inanimate (Bray 2009:358).

In addition to the calendrical functions they may have had, the 328 or so *huacas* surrounding Cusco (Bauer 1998; Zuidema 1964) must have served as powerful protectors of the Inca state. They were a standing army and a council of wise advisors always in residence.

Caves, Water, and the Sun

The origin myth that was central to the Inca state involves the emergence of the first Inca, Manco Capac, his brothers, and their sisters-wives from a cave called Tambo Tocco near Pacariqtambo. According to Sarmiento de Gamboa there were three caves. Manco Capac traveled to Cusco and conquered the people of the area (Urton 1990). Another origin myth describes how the creator god, Viracocha, caused the sun and moon to rise from the waters of Lake Titicaca, ending darkness on the earth. A shrine, the Sacred Rock, on the Island of the Sun marks that place of emergence and became one of the great pilgrimage centers of the Inca Empire. The important mytho-historic symbolism of the origins of the Inca Empire are movement upward from a cave or a body of water, the number three, the conquering of darkness by the sun, and triumph of order over chaos. These symbols recur in various manifestations in most of the ceremonial centers and *huaca* sanctuaries of the Inca.

Intihuatanas

Bingham identified the carved stone adjacent to the Urubamba River as an *intihuatana*, probably guided by local informants. He wrote prominently of the more famous *intihuatana* above the river in Machu Picchu.

> *Inti* means "sun" and *huatana* is "a place where animals are tied." The *intihuatana* would seem to be "the place to which the sun was tied," so that it could not escape. A primitive folk, so extremely dependent on the kindly behavior of the sun as were the Peruvian highlanders, must have been in terror each year as the shadows lengthened and the sun went farther and farther north, that it would never return but would leave them to perish of cold and hunger. Hence it seems likely that these short stone posts represented the post to which a mystical rope was tied by the priests to prevent the sun from going too far away and getting lost (Bingham 1952).

There are differing interpretations regarding the purpose meant for these "hitching posts of the sun." Bingham's explanation seems plausible, but other suggestions that the carvings were devised as astronomical sighting devices are not supported. Although often identified by tour guides as a calendrical shadow-casting gnomon, there is really no evidence that the *Intihuatana* stone of Machu Picchu was used for observing and establishing dates of the solstices or even the zenith sun. We strongly suggest in Chapter Five that it is a replica of Huayna Picchu, but it simply may be a fine example of Inca sculpture and art that resulted in the animation of the stone and creation of a *huaca.*

Ceremonial center of Pisac. G. Ziegler diagram.

Intihuatanas are also found at Pisac and Tipon. In Pisac the *intihuatana* is a large, partially carved rock in the temple group that is enclosed by a semicircular masonry wall adjoining a straight masonry wall. It displays a stone gnomon on its flat upper surface within the walled enclosure. Squier (1877) was informed by the governor of Pisac that this gnomon had once been clad with a bronze sheath. The primary rock extends beneath and beyond the wall of the structure where a second gnomon is located.

The *Intihuatana* of Tipon exhibits a different style, in that the in situ rock remains in a natural state and a platform has been built around it. The June solstice sunset can be viewed over the *intihuatana* from a vantage point in the vicinity of the fifth terrace and its neighboring storehouse.

Double-Jamb Doorways

In the Inca world, special doorways within doorways—double-jamb—mark the entry into the residences of elites and powerful ceremonial places. We can distinguish three types of such doorways:

1) Entry into elite residences
2) Entry into sacred and ceremonial spaces
3) A doorway for the sun

Uncleared double-jamb entrance at Choquequirao.
Hugh Thomson photo.

Solar and Ceremonial Double-Jamb Doorways			
	Location	Faces	
1	Llactapata	June solstice sunrise	
2	Coricancha	June solstice sunrise	
3	Machu Picchu: Conjunto 1	June solstice sunrise	
4	Choquequirao		Entry to *usnu*
5	Moray	December solstice sunrise	
6	Ollantaytambo	June solstice sunrise	
7	Tipon		Entry to *intihuatana*
8	Quespiwanka: Palace of Huayna Capac in Urubamba	December solstice sunrise	Triple Jamb; entry to courtyard
9	Sondor		Two doorways, at the bottom and top of stairway, leading to *huaca* on summit.

Near dawn of the June solstice the rays of the sun reach deep beyond the door, where perhaps a celebrant would greet the sun. One of the most famous solar doorways is that in the Coricancha, which faces June solstice sunrise and opens the courtyard containing halls dedicated to the sun, moon, rainbow, and thunder. A similar double-jamb doorway faces June solstice sunrise at Llactapata.

Water and Camay

Running water, as previously mentioned, is an important energizing and animating life force in Andean cultures known

June solstice illumination at Llactapata. Carlos Aranibar photo.

as "*camay.*" The agent of camay, the "*camayer*" is known as *camac* (Bray 2009; Malville 2009; Salomon and Urioste 1991). The dark constellation of the Celestial Llama is the *camac* of llamas, responsible for giving llamas the vitality to flourish on the earth. The Pleiades, also known as the storehouse or granary *(colca)*, was especially revered because that asterism was considered the supreme *camac*, or the mother from which flowed all the energy for animals (Cobo 1983:30).

It seems quite possible that the sun was understood to be a *camac* for certain *huacas*, such as the rocks of the Torreon and the Sun Temple at Llactapata, which are touched by light of the rising sun at June solstice. People skilled in their crafts, such as sculptors, engineers, and weavers would be *camayers*. As early as 600 CE, drainage canals in Tiwanaku may have served the ritual purpose of energizing sacred buildings through the process of *camay* (Couture 2004). We find evidence for similar energizing of sacred buildings at Machu Picchu, where the canal was diverted toward the *huaca* of the Torreon/Royal Mausoleum. At Tipon, the major aqueduct was diverted under its *intihuatana* and the Ceremonial Plaza.

Ceques and Huacas of Cusco

The most detailed descriptions of Inca astronomy by the Spanish chroniclers involve the solar pillars of Cusco, where as many as sixteen pillars on the horizon once marked the annual changes in the location of the rising or setting sun (Aveni 1981; Bauer and Dearborn 1995; Zuidema 1991). None of the pillars that were on the Cusco horizon has survived the Spanish campaign of eradication of indigenous cosmology and religion. On sunrise of the feast day of June solstice, Inca Inti Raymi and his relatives watched the rising sun from the plaza of Haucaypata, Plaza de Armas, while others watched the event from the Plaza Cusipata, to the west across the Huatanay River. After drinking to the Sun, the celebrants on the *usnu* poured *chicha* and/or water from Lake Titicaca into a basin from which the liquid flowed in a channel to the House of the Sun (Bauer 2004; Zuidema 1991).

The horizon pillars on the surrounding horizon and the *usnu* in the plaza of Cusco were important features of Inca ceremonialism in Cusco, but it seems likely that the most powerful ritual objects in the Cusco basin were the 328 or so *huacas* tied together by 41 *ceques* that radiated outward from the Coricancha, the principal sun temple in Cusco (Bauer 1998; Zuidema 1964). The personhood of these *huacas* may have been of primary significance because they may have been understood to be powerful protectors of the capital of the Inca Empire and valued sources of advice and wisdom for the Inca.

The Sanctuary of Isla del Sol
A State-Sponsored Pilgrimage Center

Together with the Coricancha and the coastal pilgrimage center Pachacamac, the Island of the Sun and Island of the Moon in Lake Titicaca were the most important *huacas* of the Inca Empire. In particular, the sanctuary containing the Sacred Rock, Titicala, located on the northern end of Isla del Sol in Lake Titicaca was a major state-sponsored pilgrimage center.

Within Inca origin myths, the Sun, and therefore the first Inca, Manco Capac, had first emerged from the Sacred Rock surrounded as it is by the waters of Lake Titicaca (Bauer and Stanish 2001; Dearborn et al. 1998). The sanctuary appears to have been a *huaca* before the creation of the Inca Empire and became a major ritual center during the Tiwanaku Period, 400–1200 CE. Formalized pilgrimage occurred most likely around the time of June solstice. There are markers on the horizon at the sanctuary indicating the position of the setting sun at June solstice. Something similar may have been present before it became an Inca pilgrimage center.

The difficult journey to the island and along its spine gave it a sense of otherworldliness and liminality for the pilgrims. The several checkpoints along the route controlled access to the sanctuary. The concave portion of the Sacred Rock was reportedly covered by gold and silver and the entire rock was sometimes clothed by a large, finely woven cloth (Bauer and Stanish 2001). The clothing of the rock is consistent with the belief in the living nature of a *huaca* (Bray 2009).

The first European visitors to the area reported numerous women attendants who made large quantities of corn beer (*chicha*), which was poured into a stone basin at the base of the sacred rock. The basin had a hole in its center and stone-lined channels carried the *chicha* away from the rock. *Chicha* maintained the living nature of the *huaca.*

Shaped *huaca* stone at Saihuite. G. Ziegler photo.

We suggest that Machu Picchu and Choquequirao may have also been utilized as pilgrimage destinations. The long pilgrimage pathway from Cusco to Choquequirao may have passed Machu Picchu and continued onto the treacherous face of Machu Picchu Peak. The dangerous nature of that path gives it the quality of liminality often found in pilgrimage paths, like the route to Isla del Sol (Bauer and Stanish 2001). From Llactapata, the days-long route drops into the Santa Teresa Valley, climbs over Yanama Pass at 15,321 feet elevation, then descends the Yanama Valley to finally climb back up to enter

Choquequirao. The first view is truly spectacular, similar to that from the *Intipunku*—the Sun Gate—above Machu Picchu. The ceremonial *usnu* platform seen from above is a remarkable sight.

The Ridge Top Shrine: Special Huaca to Apu Huaca Huilca

A small herder's trail climbs diagonally up some 3,200 feet from the Urubamba River canyon several miles downriver from Ollantaytambo to a prominent ridge top. The remains of a stone-lined Inca trail built along the ridge is evident. A tall double-jamb gateway and wall sets on a platform on the crest of a small summit of the ridge retained on two sides by low, fieldstone walls. A short, six-foot wide stairway leads up to the left side of the gate to a small, walled platform in front. One can then walk through to a larger, walled, semicircular platform on the opposite side.

Ridge top shrine above Choqueticarpo and the Ollantaytambo quarries

G. Ziegler photo.

Inside, a 13-foot high wall with two small niches and a tall "stand-in" niche in the center extend out from one side of the gateway. Below the niche closest to the ending edge of the wall is a stone with drilled holes indicating that something probably was attached here, perhaps decorative cloth or metal. The Torreon at Machu Picchu has similar holes.

Drilled holes at ridge top shrine. G. Ziegler photo.

The view from inside the gateway is spectacular. The slope plunges steeply to the depths of the Silque Canyon to the west some 3,200 feet below. The massive canyon of the Urubamba and the ice peaks of the Urubamba Range dominate the foreground. Farther along the ridge, another flattened crest appears to be a platform or *usnu* overlooking the Urubamba, which would have a direct sightline upriver toward Ollantaytambo.

View of Veronica (Huaca Huilca) through double-jamb gateway. G. Ziegler photo.

Viewed through the gateway, the majestic glacier and cloud-enshrouded summit of the ice peak, Veronica, or Huaca Huilca as it is traditionally known, is framed and centered. Johan Reinhard (2002) describes the regional importance of this sacred mountain (*apu*), the highest and most prominent feature observable from Machu Picchu. We measured the alignment and corresponding sightline focus to the peak to be directly north.

From the prominent lofty location and easterly view, we expected to find a *huaca* with solstice alignments in the direction of Ollantaytambo or something like the *intipunku* gate on the approach to Machu Picchu. Instead, we examined a very special mountain *huaca* and shrine very probably dedicated to the power and magnificence of a spiritually great mountain. Reinhard and others have written that the Vilcanota River, or Urubamba as it is called here, was the Andean metaphorical embodiment of the celestial river, the Milky Way. The occurrence of the mountain and sacred river viewed together from the platform must have had unusual significance for those who visited and attended the shrine (Reinhard 2002).

Five
Astronomy and the Sacred Landscape of Choquequirao

As previously mentioned, boulders, springs, caves, weather, celestial phenomena, and in particular mountains and rivers, were embodied with supernatural powers. Daily routine involved various rituals to honor, influence, or appease these living forces. The Inca imposed a highly ritualized, state-sponsored, sun cult on top of and incorporating these ancient, traditional beliefs. American anthropologists Brian Bauer and Charles Stanish have suggested that the Inca invested in major pilgrimage sites to impress the population.

Sunrise on June 21st from the *usnu*. Humberto Medrano photo.

The Isla del Sol Sanctuary appears to provide a basic plan for pilgrimage centers: separation of class into upper and lower status, gateways, offerings of *chicha* to the sun poured into an altar with stone-lined channels and the presence of water. The route to the sanctuary had several gates and checkpoints to control entry to the area. On the mainland, before reaching Copacabana, pilgrims had to pass through gates where they were inspected by guards. After traveling by boat to the island, pilgrims would walk northward to the sanctuary.

Most pilgrims were prevented from entering the actual sanctuary by another gateway, known as the *Intipunku*—door of the Sun—where they handed offerings to attendants. The ceremonies at the Sacred Rock could have been watched by lower-status pilgrims from a platform perhaps 325 yards distant. Ceremonies involved watching the setting of the June solstice sun between two pillars on the horizon (Bauer and Stanish 2001). Incorporating some of these same aspects, Choquequirao may have functioned as a regional pilgrimage

View toward June solstice sunrise from the lower plaza at Choquequirao. G. Ziegler photo.

View toward the Apurimac and June solstice sunset point. G. Ziegler photo.

center. The upper *usnu* is reached only after passing through a double-jamb doorway. The lower plaza may have been the place for lower-status pilgrims. A stone-lined water channel is a prominent feature of the place.

From our project work at Llactapata, Machu Picchu's ceremonial neighbor and sun temple, we have learned to look carefully at alignments and interrelated feature placements. As example, an entranceway, window, or corridor facing northeast is probable indication of a June solstice alignment.[15] The

View from the Giant Staircase toward the December solstice sunrise. G. Ziegler photo.

Humberto Medrano photo.

mid-June sun rises over Machu Picchu as seen from the Llactapata temple at an azimuth of 64.3 degrees (Malville, Thomson, and Ziegler 2004; Thomson 2006).

December Solstice Alignment

Several important features at Choquequirao face or focus upon the horizon point where sunrise occurs during the December

Paolo Greer photo.

solstice. The Principal Temple's multiple doorways on the west side of the Lower Plaza face outward at 112 degrees, the angle of the first appearance of the sun at 7 degrees elevation on the horizon around mid-December. The triangular-shaped main or Lower Plaza is aligned to face the December solstice sunrise. The long, open, Apurimac-facing retaining wall lies on the perpendicular to 112 degrees, The large, main *kallanca's* entrances face outward at 112 degrees.

The large group of storage houses (*colcas*), several long, large buildings, and associated parallel-aligned smaller structures located mid-way between the Upper and Lower Plaza also face outward toward the upper Apurimac Canyon and

Solstice alignment of the Lower Plaza group. Paolo Greer photo.

the December solstice sunrise. However, they are off a few degrees from a precise, solstice alignment along with the nearby narrow, side-walled, descending terraces, which Hiram Bingham named "The Giant Staircase." The outward view-line is 120–125 degrees (m). Although certainly placed to view the rising sun and Apurimac Canyon, they probably did not have a solstice-ceremonial purpose like the Lower Plaza, temple, and water features below.

June Solstice Alignment

From the Lower Plaza and the *usnu* platform, the June solstice sunrise can be seen near a distinct pointed rock formation at 57 degrees.[16] The center entranceway of the semi-round fountain group faces outward at 65 degrees—the close, approximate azimuth of the June solstice sunrise.

May sunrise from the fountains group, the Lower Plaza. Ken Greenwood photo.

Viewed from the higher *usnu* platform, the June solstice sun sets at 293 degrees near the summit of the ice peak, Nevado Panta. The December sun rises over a point looking up the Apurimac gorge to the southeast. This suggests a potent convergence of spiritually important geographical features—the "talking god," or Apurimac River, and a sacred glacier-topped mountain (*apu*).

Replication Stones

Connected to and above the Giant Staircase is a small plaza hosting a large, irregularly shaped boulder. When viewed from the north, the rock closely replicates the southern horizon on the far side of the Apurimac. If so, this is a significant discovery from our most recent 2013 visit. We had written that Choquequirao has no replication stones like Machu Picchu because of the nature of the difficulty to shape, in situ, metamorphic rock, whereas the fine-grained granite of Machu Picchu allows easy sculpturing and shaping. Reflecting a focus on mountain worship and sacred geography, the site abounds in boulders, many enshrined by walls, shaped to replicate the rugged surrounding

Shaped stone at Choquequirao. G. Ziegler photo.

horizon and individual distant peaks. The stones represent one of many sacred and spiritually empowered natural objects and forces—*huacas* that influenced life and beliefs in the Andes. It is predictable that Choquequirao would have them as well.

Notes

15. A first step in examining a newly found structure is to determine its size, form, and alignment. After initial machete clearing for access, alignment of entrances, windows, and walls is determined with a surveying compass. We learn much about mountain Inca sites by structural designs indicative of function in conjunction with angles of view and probable sightline focus. The general layout of a group or compound is determined and initially evaluated as well. A rule of thumb is to sight directly out an entranceway or window at the angle of view. Knowing the magnetic azimuths for important Inca events like solstice sunrise and sunset calculated for foreground elevation is necessary. As example, a 50-yard long walled corridor at Llactapata looks out toward the center of Machu Picchu some 2 miles away at an angle of 64.3 degrees, the angle of June solstice sunrise on the distant horizon, and close to the rise of the important constellation Pleiades at 67 degrees. A reasonable interpretation is that the corridor was intended to view these important events when they appeared over Machu Picchu. This and other evidence allowed us to conclude that this was a feature of a temple of the sun similar to the Coricancha in Cusco.

16. At the Coricancha in Cusco, important sun events like the solstices were calculated by stone marker towers that defined the sun's movement on the distant horizon. (Bauer and Dearborn 1995; Zuidema 1964). Kim Malville has recently identified similar towers defining the sun's movement on a high ridge northeast of the town of Urubamba, which were probably placed as a feature of Huayna Capac's estate located there.

Six
Machu Picchu's Sacred Landscape and Design, A Model for Choquequirao

Overview of the main groups at Machu Picchu. G. Ziegler diagram.

Noted Andean anthropologist John Rowe (1990) wrote that Machu Picchu was built as a royal estate of the Inca Pachacuti, induced from a sixteenth-century document and other compelling evidence. Carefully placed by Inca design, South America's famous and most visited ancient city is spectacularly situated on a cloud-forested, granite-spine ridge some 1,500 feet above a deeply incised meander of the Urubamba River. The similarity with Choquequirao is striking. We believe that

Machu Picchu was located, designed, and functioned as a ceremonial center incorporating the site's unique convergence of geographical features—sacred mountains and the Urubamba River—with astronomical and geo-cosmic alignments.

Our observation is that every feature or construction appears to be planned and aligned with purpose, leaving nothing to chance. Archaeoastronomer David Dearborn and others have identified structures, building groups, and features oriented to focus upon, point to, or replicate geographical features, solar alignment, and other astronomical phenomena (Dearborn 1981; Reinhard 2002; Wright and Valencia 2001). We have further identified features and groups seemingly associated with solstice alignment or the surrounding mountains—Huayna Picchu, Cerro Machu Picchu, Yanatin, San Miguel, Cerro Putucusi, and the Llactapata groups. The alignment of Salkantay, one of the traditionally sacred mountains, with the Pleiades, dark constellations, Milky Way, and the Southern Cross is particularly significant at Machu Picchu (Reinhard 2002).

The multiplicity of different ceremonial features and groups within the city indicate that it probably hosted a complex schedule of ritual events, celebrations, and important gatherings throughout the Inca calendar. The predominance of mountain replication shrines and solstice alignments suggest that the primary spiritual focus at Machu Picchu was mountain worship and the sun. This city estate appears to have been a complex, busy urban center incorporating different purposes with multiple levels of ceremonial and utilitarian usage before its decline and abandonment sometime before or during the arrival of the European invaders in Cusco in 1533.

A major road network connecting extensive Inca-controlled regions to the west—Vitcos and Choquequirao—reinforces the idea that Machu Picchu was a spiritual and administrative hub of a network of roads, regional settlements, and state-controlled commerce (Kendall 1988). A large staging area and meeting hall outside the city wall and a number of internal

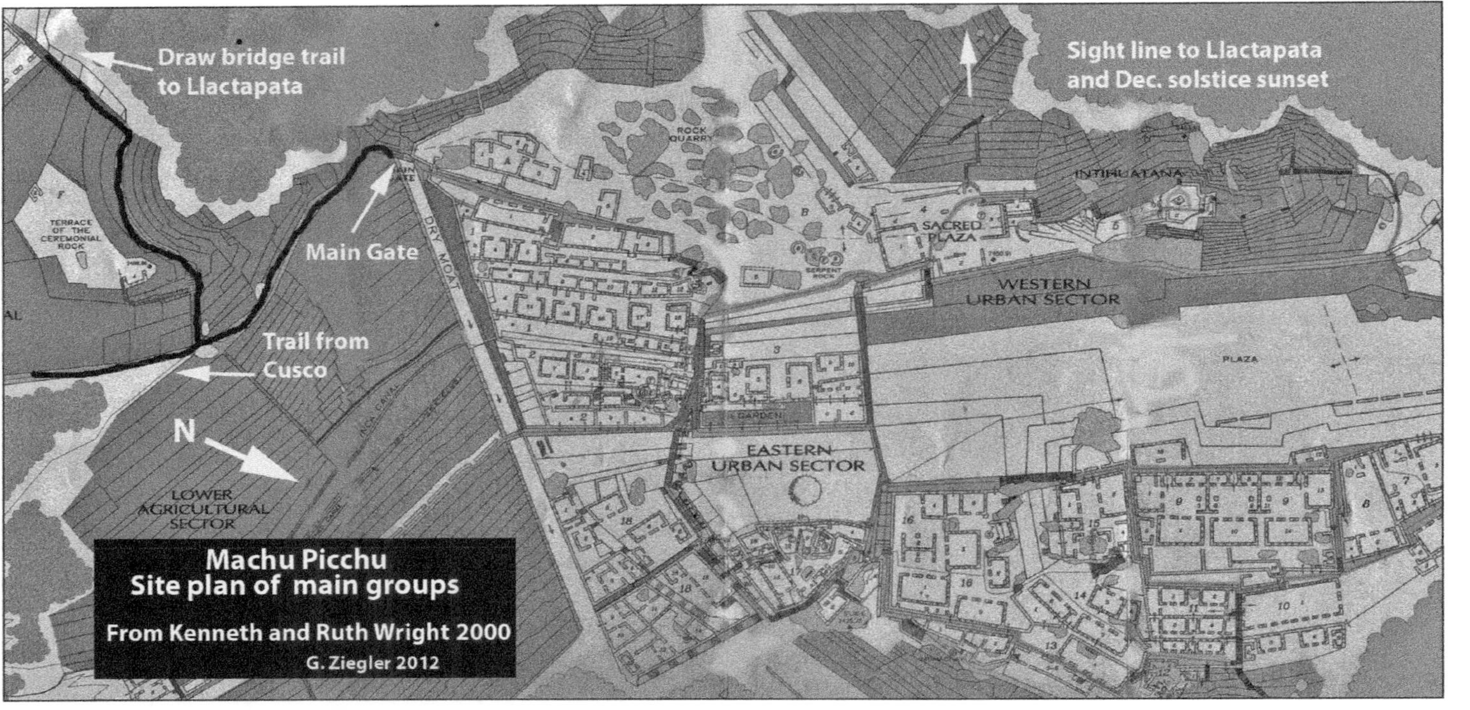

Site plan map of Machu Picchu. Kenneth and Ruth Wright diagram.

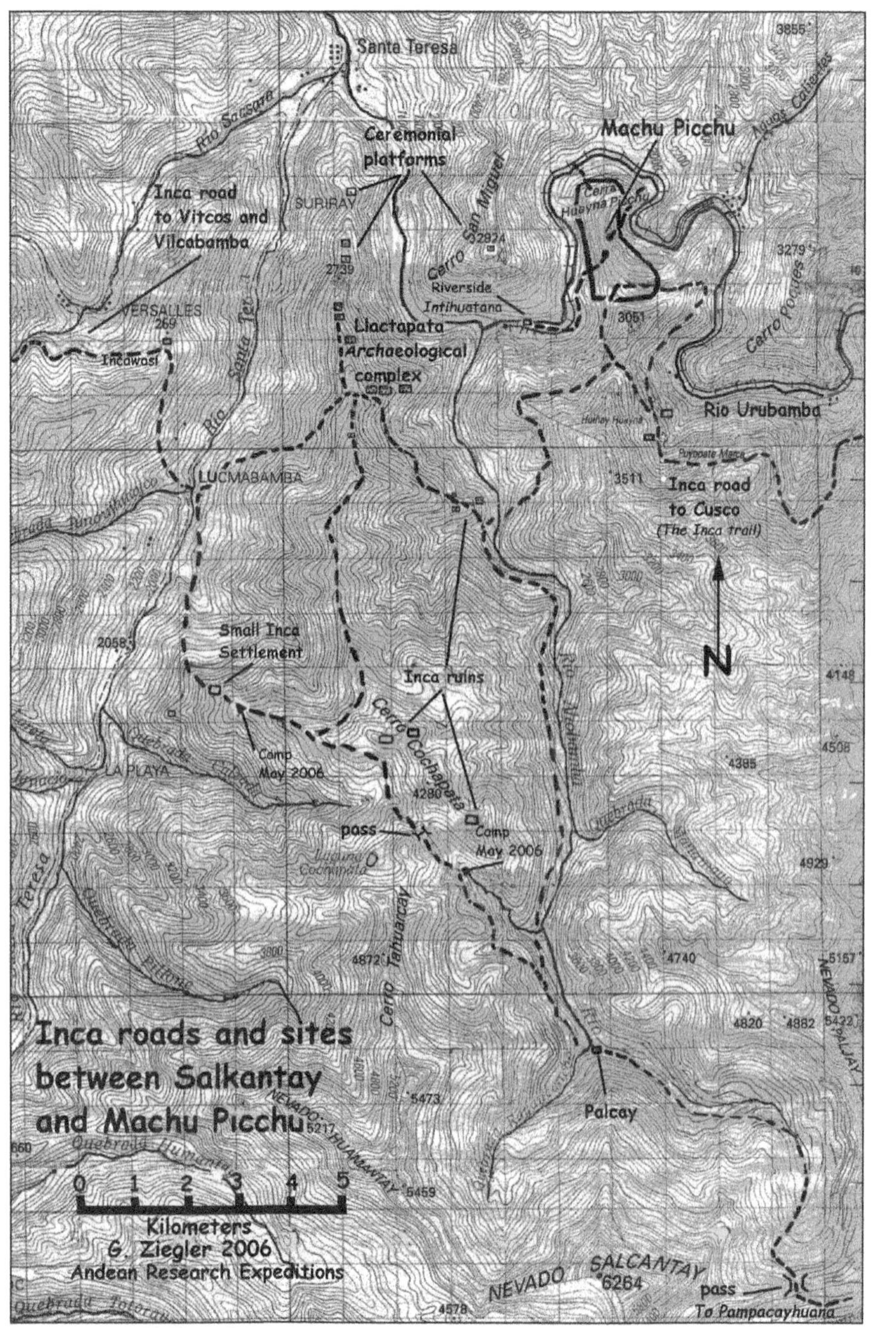

Regional map of Inca roads and sites. G. Ziegler diagram.

warehouses *(colcas)* indicate that the site may have been a collecting point for goods arriving from the Vilcabamba to be sent on to the capital or for other distribution.

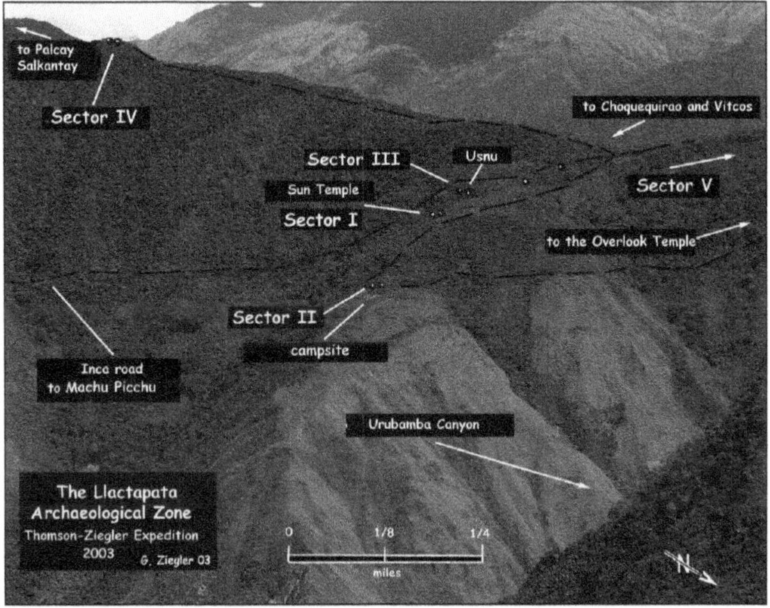

Photo map of Llactapata from Huayna Picchu. G. Ziegler photo.

In 2003, exploratory investigations by the Royal Geographical Society–supported Thomson-Ziegler expedition revealed the relationships and importance of a large complex of ruins associated with Machu Picchu at nearby Llactapata. The project identified a temple of the sun, modeled after the Coricancha in Cusco, a group of buildings associated with water features, and a large rectangular *usnu* platform. The continuation of the Inca road or trail from Machu Picchu onward into the Vilcabamba was located and mapped. A second branch was later documented southward up the Aobamba Valley to the site of Palcay and beyond (Malville, Thomson, and Ziegler 2004; Ziegler 2007).

We have shown that numbers of imported workers *(Mitimae)* lived near Choquequirao, Cotacoca, and Corihuayrachina

(Cerro Victoria) in small wood-sided and simple stone hut settlements (Ziegler 1999, 2002). Explorations at Llactapata revealed a similar, sizable, low-status settlement and agricultural fields located within several hours of Machu Picchu on the nearby Aobamba-Santa Teresa Ridge. The area would have provided a resident pool of laborers (Malville, Thomson, and Ziegler 2004).

British archaeologist Ann Kendall (1984) writes that the large Cusichaca site, Patallacta, east of Machu Picchu, may have also served in part as a resident settlement of laborers for Machu Picchu. Anthropologists Susan Niles and Maria Rostworowski have demonstrated that some royal estates functioned as administrative centers for the surrounding region. It is reasonable to assume that Machu Picchu and Choquequirao would have also served as such (Niles 1999; Rostworowski 1983; Rowe 1990).

Geo-Cosmic Designs and Alignments

A complete description of Machu Picchu is beyond the scope of this book. We limit discussions to a few important aspects that convey the essence of design and probable purposes of Pachacuti's unique estate in association with nearby Llactapata. Machu Picchu is distinguished from other royal estates in the Inca heartland by a large multiplicity of *huacas* and an overwhelmingly powerful spiritual location offering a retreat of great power, comfort, and security. Pachacuti surrounded his personal country retreat with a remarkable cluster of powerful *apus* and protective *huacas.* Topa Inca Yupanki chose to similarly build his own principal estate in just the same way—in a spiritually powerful location overlooking the deep Apurimac gorge at Choquequirao. The father had set a high standard for the ambitious and successful son to follow.

Terrace of the Ceremonial Rock and the Guard House

The Inca roads accessing Machu Picchu from Cusco and Ollantaytambo and from the Vilcabamba by Llactapata meet at

G. Ziegler photo.

a large, wide, terraced plaza outside the main gate of Machu Picchu. A long meeting hall *(kallanca)*, Machu Picchu's largest building, is here. A special *kallanca* located outside of Cusco served as a sort of greeting and leaving shrine to travelers coming and going from the city (Zuidema, personal communication). The *kallanca* strategically located just outside Machu Picchu's main gateway at the junction of the two main roads may have served a similar purpose.

A large shaped stone *(huaca)*, which seems to closely replicate visually prominent Cerro Yanatin, dominates the center of the plaza. A well-made single structure that Hiram Bingham called The Guard House, a *wayrona*-style building designed with one side open, faces toward the rock and plaza. It is similar to two buildings that border the Sacred Rock Plaza inside the city and probably served a similar ritual purpose. Numbers of small, elongated stones, roughly one foot by six inches in size, are arranged in upright groups around the shaped *huaca* (Guard House). The stones are andesite, limestone, and metamorphic rock carried in from other regions. Some are rounded river-shaped rocks. Ruth Wright and Alfredo Valencia (2001) write "river rocks symbolically bring the sacred river to the mountain site." This may have been the case, but the diversity of rocks more likely indicates that they were ritual offerings or burdens carried and placed by visitors at a shine requiring this ritual upon arrival at Machu Picchu.

Modern Quechua travelers carry small stones to the top of mountain passes to leave as offerings (personal observation). Visitors to the Sapa Inca and the Coricancha in Cusco were reported to have carried burdens. Travelers left stones at roadside shrines, called *apachitas* (Cieza 1967; Garcilaso 1987). The plaza and buildings were likely a staging area for llama trains, supplies, labor gangs, workers, warehouse goods, and state business coming and going.

A ceremonial area located outside the gate with a replication of Cerro Yanatin suggests that Yanatin (Yanati) may have had special importance to travelers along these main routes and to those not allowed inside the inner city. Additionally, ceremonies may have been held here for lower-status workers and neighboring settlements during important calendar events. Large amounts of broken pottery have been found here, suggesting ritual drinking activities (Wright and Valencia 2001).

Main Gate and Entrance Corridor

In various cultures around the world, sacred architecture has been used to guide the ritual movement of people as well as to limit their field of view. Archaeologist John Fritz (1978) argues that ceremonial structures and city planning are occasionally designed to provide earthly parallels to the cosmos, reinforcing the ideological integration of a society as its social stratification. Only those with access to certain esoteric knowledge, such as the location of sunrise, the presence of a god in a temple or natural topographic feature, or the symbolic meaning of a mountain, could design such structures, thereby confirming their high status in the society.

While performing rituals, participants are forced to follow certain pathways and view certain perspectives, such as sacred mountains, palaces, or temples. Fritz suggests sites in India and Chaco Canyon in the American Southwest as examples of such ritual architecture.

The entrance corridor at Machu Picchu appears to be another excellent example of such architecture and planning. This impressive gateway frames and focuses attention upon Cerro Huayna Picchu. A narrow, walled corridor leads inward some distance, viewing Huayna Picchu when entering, framing Cerro Machu Picchu when exiting. Soon turning sharply to the right, the corridor passes through a second gateway framing distant Cerro Putucusi. Following yet another turn and gateway, the walkway continues downward to the Sacred Plaza and heart of the complex.

The focus on principal mountain features surrounding Machu Picchu with passage through monumental gates, each defining a new focus, suggest the pathway as a walkway utilized for important ritual processions, as well as an ascetic and impressive architectural design for utilitarian passage. A first focus upon Huayna Picchu gives prime importance to the site's most prominent mountain feature.

Solstice Alignments

A number of groups and features distributed throughout Machu Picchu are aligned with the June solstice sunrise azimuth of approximately 61–62 degrees. The December solstice sunrise azimuth is approximately 112 degrees, with the sun setting

G. Ziegler photo.

at 245 degrees corrected for elevation of the distant horizon. The abundance of structures facing these directions, along with the known importance of the solstice ceremonies to the Inca state sun cult, strongly suggest solstice worship as a primary design purpose.

The Sacred Plaza

The Sacred Plaza is enclosed on three sides, open to the west, with an alignment of 243–245 degrees. The House of Three

Windows forms the easterly side opening on the plaza facing Llactapata and the distant summit of Nevado Pumasillo, a mountain sacred to the Inca (Reinhard 2002).

June solstice sunrise would be seen at 62 degrees from the three windows rising over the distant Cordillera Urubamba. During the December solstice, the sun would be seen to set over Llactapata and Pumasillo at 245 degrees. A well-made semi-circular wall and platform resembling a similar wall at the Coricancha in Cusco is complementary to and symmetrical with the curved wall of the Torreon and its view of June solstice sunrise. It faces the Sun Temple at Llactapata and the December solstice sunset. A shaped stone at the platform appears to replicate the Llactapata topography.

Sacristy Temple. Paolo Greer photo.

The magnificently constructed Sacristy temple, a few steps from the platform, also faces Llactapata at 245 degrees. It contains two remarkable polygonal stones with 32 angles, a stone bench facing southwest, and 13 niches (Reinhard 2002; Wright and Valancia 2001). With an orientation of 245 degrees, its long axis is perpendicular to the direction to the sun temple at Llactapata. From the entrance, or from the stone bench within, one can look directly into the Llactapata sun temple. In addition,

Replica stone of Llactapata ridge. G. Ziegler photo.

Circular wall facing Llactapata. G. Ziegler photo.

the December solstice sun can be seen setting near the snow peak of Pumasillo (Reinhard 2002).

One of the important roles of Llactapata could have been signaling the June solstice sunrise. June solstice sunrise, reflected by a mirror at Llactapata, arrives there 36 minutes before it does at Machu Picchu. That would give solar priests stationed in the Sacristy sufficient time to move out to the Sacred Plaza, the Torreon, and the *Intihuatana* to bring up the sun. Best of all, they may have announced the impending sunrise with the blowing of conchs and the start of chanting. What an impressive demonstration of the power of the Inca. To the east of the Sacristy and north of the Sacred Plaza is a *huaca,* a large tilted stone embedded in the terraces and walls. It has steps leading to its top, which would have provided views to the east and west, and it may have been climbed by a celebrant to announce solstice sunrise.

The three window building on Huayna Picchu faces Llactapata and contains a replica stone of the Llactapata ridge.

Sun mirror reflection from Llactapata. Carlos Aranibar photo.

Celebrants in that building who watched Llactapata for a signal would also be able to move to the summit of Huayna Picchu to observe the solstice sunrise.

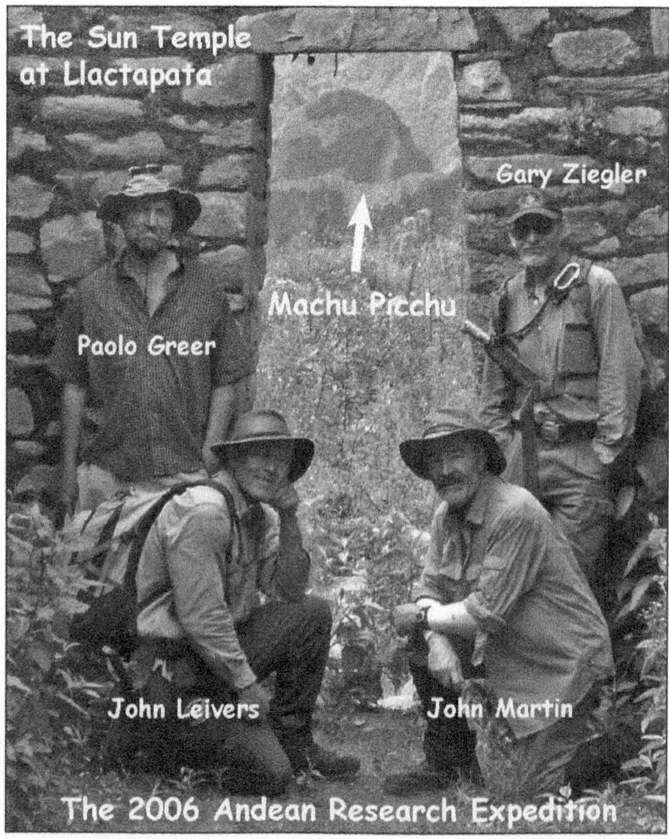

John Martin photo.

Intihuatana

The *Intihuatana* platform, or *usnu,* has a six-foot-plus high wall structure on the south side with an entranceway now partially filled, and remains of a wall on the east. The east wall is gone but the foundation is evident. The alignment indicated by the perpendicular from the east wall and the parallel of the south wall creates a sightline angle of 245 degrees from the open west side to Llactapata and the main summit of Nevado

Gary Ziegler at Machu Picchu 1965. G. Ziegler photo.

Machu Picchu *Intihuatana.* G. Ziegler photo.

Pumasillo on the far horizon, also the December solstice setting azimuth. Shaped stones on the walkway up from the south and the Sacred Plaza appear to replicate the eastern horizon representing Cerros Yanati and Putucusi. The main *huaca* stone, the *Intihuatana*, viewed from the southern approaching steps, strongly appears to replicate Huayna Picchu, which imposingly dominates the northern view. The solstice alignment suggests that this was a primary ceremonial consideration of this central *huaca.*

The *usnu* platform offers a breathtaking 360-degree view. Reinhard and others have noted that important mountains lie at cardinal directions from the platform, the most important being Salkantay, located directly south at 180 degrees, with Veronica to the east.

The *usnu* is well suited for celestial activities. The hilltop location makes the platform an exceptional place to make astrological observations in association with sacred geography (Reinhard 2002). It is likely that a number of ceremonies and celestial observations were performed here throughout the year. The alignment of several important groups and the focus of the main entranceway upon Huayna Picchu suggest that this mountain was the principal and protectorate deity, or *apu,* of Machu Picchu. The *Intihuatana* stone as a replication of Huayna Picchu and the number of ceremonial features on the mountain itself strengthens the case. The *Intihuatana* is the central and most important shrine located on the principal raised platform, or *usnu,* above the Sacred Plaza, the highest point on the cities' only pyramid.

The Torreon

The Torreon is another well-known feature with a June solstice focus. Popularly called the Temple of the Sun, a shaped stone enclosed within is reported to receive a ray of sunlight through the east-facing window during the June solstice (Dearborn and White 1983; Reinhard 2002; Wright and Valencia 2001). The shaped *huaca* stone, enclosed by this unusual D-shaped build-

The Torreon with June sunrise. Carlos Aranibar photo.

ing was likely a replication stone and altar for associated rituals, llama sacrifice, and *chicha* offering.

The important June Pleiades rising (Zuidema 1982) and the June solstice could have been viewed from the east-facing window but the alignment is not precise, off by some degrees from the angle of other site solstice features. It does, however, present a centered view of the early morning rise of the Pleiades during late May and June. Dearborn and White have noted that a plumb bob hanging in the window would cast a shadow on a carved groove on the stone at June solstice, leading them to suggest that the Torreon served as a sun temple or a solar observatory.

With a rock illuminated by the June solstice sun and niches for mummies underneath, the Torreon has been the focus of most of the discussions of astronomy at Machu Picchu. It combines a cave, symbolic stairs, niches for ancestors, illumination at June solstice, and proximity to transformative water. Because of the similarity of its beautifully curving wall, it has been likened to the Coricancha of Cusco and identified as a sun temple. However, it is a unique and powerful *huaca* in its own right.

Other than the curved wall, there are few similarities with the Coricancha. The Torreon and neighboring area are tiny compared to the Coricancha, which is a large compound measuring 94 yards on its northern wall and 69 yards on the east. Its inner courtyard was approximately 39 yards on a side. The inner curved portion of the Torreon is 4 yards in diameter and the long wall adjacent to the Torreon has a length of 9 yards. The Coricancha contained at least six halls and a long corridor with a double-jamb doorway oriented toward the rising of the Pleiades and the June solstice sun. The Torreon by these standards was more like a "shrine," which in Andean culture was often a *huaca*.

The northeast window of the Torreon faces the rising of the Pleiades; the sun on June solstice is off-center. An edge of a raised portion of the rock inside the Torreon lies "within 2' ± 5' of the rising point of the sun on June solstice" (Dearborn and White 1983:249). There are several things that are odd about this feature. It is not a right angle edge, something that Inca masons would have had no difficulty with. When one puts one's eye along it, only the wall below the window is visible. Raising one's eye to the horizon means losing any precision of measurement. Dearborn and White suggest that a stick holding a plumb bob could have been mounted on the outside of the window and observers could have established the date of solstice by observing when the shadow fell along the edge.

Unfortunately, the sun at solstice is not centered in the window, and the string would have to be previously adjusted in order for its shadow to align with the rock edge. It seems like a Catch 22 situation, in which only when the position of the sun is known, can this method be used to establish the date of solstice. Furthermore, if a direct sighting to the sunrise was desired, more of the rock could have been removed to provide a direct sightline. If the Torreon was intended to function as an effective observing device for establishing solstice, the window could have been built so that the sun rose in its center at June solstice. Perhaps the real intent of the builders of the Torreon was not to build an observatory for Inca priests to gaze out but rather to establish a *huaca* in which the sun looked in, and thereby could empower and animate the *huaca* through the process of *camay.*

It is without a doubt an important ceremonial *huaca* situated within a few steps of the most important residence compound and water features. The Torreon and its associated buildings and walkways are aligned 350–170 degrees, giving a focus on Huayna Picchu and Cerro Machu Picchu. The shaped stone and the architectural alignment suggest that replication and associated mountain worship may have been a primary ceremonial function. Andean researcher Paolo Greer suggests that the Torreon was a mausoleum where a replica statue (*huaque)* of Pachacuti was placed after his death. He's found that early documents say that Pachacuti's mausoleum was at a place called Patallacta. As Machu Picchu was Pachacuti's most important estate, it may have been called Patallacta and the *huaque* was maintained there by his *panaca* (Greer 2008). As with many sites, the actual name is lost. Machu Picchu probably referred originally to the prominent regional feature now called Huayna Picchu. In any case, Machu Picchu was probably not the Inca name for the estate, nor was the Torreon Machu Picchu's temple of the sun.

The Royal Mausoleum

The Royal Mausoleum, a cave with unusually special ritual features, such as internal masonry with full-size niches, a stepped

The Royal Mausoleum. G. Ziegler photo.

motif, and a shaped *usnu* stone, forms the lower section of the large granite outcrop that the Torreon sits on. The outfacing alignment of 65 degrees is precisely toward the June solstice sunrise. This suggests sun ritual as a primary function.

This superbly crafted shrine represents the finest monumental construction in the western or upper *hanan* sector of Machu Picchu below the Sacred Plaza group. It is accessed directly from the neighboring elite compound (*cancha)*, the Royal Residence, Machu Picchu's most important residential group.[17] This suggests that the cave may have been a private shrine for the visiting Inca or highly privileged others when in residence next door. If Pachacuti's *panaca* kinship administrators did maintain a home for his mummy or *huaque* representative here, we suggest this most special *huaca* cave would have been the location.

Huayna Picchu and The Temple of the Moon

Huayna Picchu and The Temple of the Moon is a large shelter cave with masonry structures underlying a massive granite capstone, associated terraces, and several small groups of outbuildings. The location is well down Cerro Huayna Picchu some distance above the Urubamba River. Two trails access the site. One route branches off from the trail up Huayna Picchu from the main groups and descends to the cave group. The other trail climbs directly from the cave up through very airy cliffs by carved stone stairs to the summit. The trail continues below the cave down to the river after passing through a fine, double-jamb gateway. This presents yet another route into Machu Picchu.

Inside the cave, finely worked granite walls with niches and recesses face outward toward the San Miguel ridge. A large shaped stone centered inside appears to replicate the San Miguel ridge and its topographic profile when viewed from behind looking outward. Caves are known to have been important to the Inca, representing sacred places embodied with spiritual powers (D'Altroy 2003; Poma 1956; Reinhard 2002).

The replication of the San Miguel ridge and orientation of the site suggests that a ceremonial function may have been a ritual associated with Cerro San Miguel. Reinhard writes that Cerro San Miguel was important as a place to worship sacred geographical features in combination with equinox alignment. He describes a large oval *usnu* platform on the summit. Like Huayna Picchu, Cerro San Miguel is surrounded on three sides by the spiritually important Urubamba River (Reinhard 2002).

The cave also may have represented a symbolic entrance into Huayna Picchu, the estate's most important natural feature, inviting ritual events by a circular route that included a ceremonial passage from Machu Picchu to the summit, down to the cave, and back to the city. The cave contains finely crafted niches for ritual placement of mummies or representative *huaques.*

The stairway climbing above The Temple of the Moon is an explicit metaphor for movement from the cave of the underworld to the upper realms. On certain occasions the primary route for ritual ascent of the mountain may have been this stairway, starting at the Urubamba River, thereby bypass-

Double-jamb gateway below Huayna Picchu. Ruth and Ken Wright photo.

Structures in the Cave of the Moon. Ruth and Ken Wright photo.

Cave of the Moon interior view. Ruth and Ken Wright photo.

ing Machu Picchu itself. Stairs are common symbolic expressions of the ascent of sacred mountains throughout the ancient world. Ziggurats of Mesopotamia were sacred mountains reaching to the heavens with processional staircases. Many pyramids are known as symbolic mountains. Processional staircases leading to the summits of pyramids are common in the Americas. A very early example is Caral on Peru's central coast, where a staircase leads from a sunken circular plaza to the top of the Great Pyramid (Solis 2006).

A smaller cave below the main cave opens to sunset on June solstice. Peruvian archaeologist Raul Delgado and colleagues Tony de Souza and Carlos Loret de Mola documented the entry of sunlight into the cave. An intriguing discovery by Delgado's team is that sunlight from one of the windows illuminates a portion of the floor that appears to be a replica of Machu Picchu, Huayna Picchu, and the Urubamba River (personal communication, Malville 2012).

House of Three Windows

A short distance below the summit of Huayna Picchu, the walkway passes through the only building on the upper portion of the mountain—the House of Three Windows. This house is a typical two-story Inca design with internal niches, trapezoidal doorways, and a gabled roof set carefully on a leveled platform built out on a filled retaining wall from the near-vertical granite slope. The interesting features are three identical tall windows looking out toward Llactapata. The walls and windows are aligned at an azimuth of 230 degrees (m) creating a direct focus line and alignment upon the main sectors of Llactapata. The group centered at the spring (the only water source) that we have designated as Llactapata Sector II is aligned to face Huayna Picchu at 50 degrees (the back azimuth of 230).

A number of other ceremonial features at the House of Three Windows focus on Huayna Picchu (Malville, Thomson, and Ziegler 2004). A shaped replica stone resembling the profile of the ridge and its facing topography sets in front of the

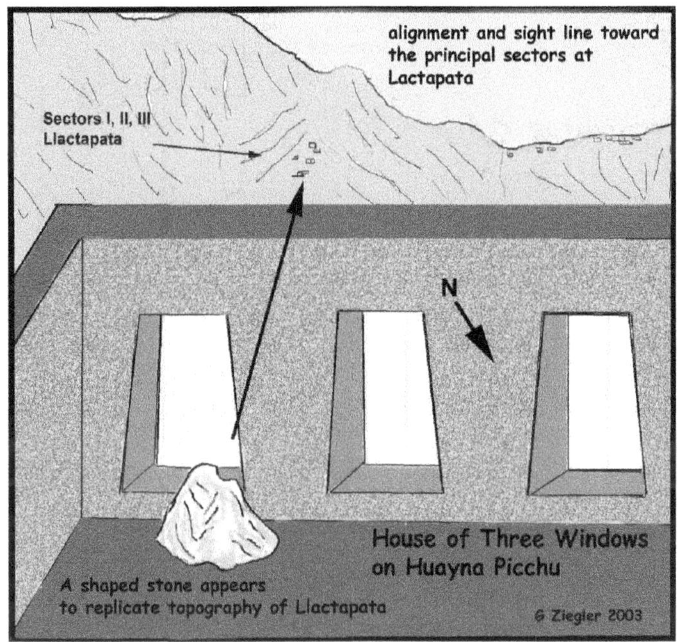

Drawing of the House of Three Windows. G. Ziegler diagram.

left window allowing the viewer to view the distant ridge and its replication at the same time. The alignment directly toward the Llactapata sites and the shaped replication stone suggest that the house was a shrine or *huaca* focusing on and emphasizing a special reciprocal spiritual importance between Llactapata and Huayna Picchu.[18]

Temple of the Condor

A carved condor head in bedrock is below two rock formations that look like wings. The point or beak aligns outward at 112 degrees facing the December solstice sunrise. In the cave at the rear are a series of steps, which do not appear to go anywhere. James Westerman photographed the light of the rising sun on August 19, 1995, when it had a declination of 12048′ and passed between two buildings, touched the head of the condor, and entered the cave beyond it. He also documented the event on April 21, 1994.

Annotated view of Huayna Picchu and Machu Picchu from Llactapata. G. Ziegler photo.

The Condor Rock. G. Ziegler photo.

Tom Zuidema has noted that August 18 was a major festival for the Inca associated with planting, during which large numbers of guinea pigs were sacrificed, partly because it was believed that they would otherwise turn into toads. He found that August 18 was the day of the anti-zenith sun, when the sun at midnight was precisely at the nadir. More significantly that day, when the sun has a declination equal to the latitude, and the day of the zenith sun (when the sun has a declination equal to the negative of the latitude) were symmetrically located relative to the equinox. Because of the importance of symmetry to the Inca, Zuidema proposed that these two dates were important in their ceremonial calendar and could readily be determined by observing the locations of respective sunrises and sunsets[19] (Zuidema 1991).

The combination of condor and anti-zenith sun suggests the symbolism of the three worlds. Just to the south of the Temple of the Condor is a large building in which the ground floor was used for raising guinea pigs. It contains guinea pig hutches in which ancient droppings were found. If the Temple of the Condor was a place for celebrations on August 18–19, when guinea pigs were sacrificed elsewhere in the Inca Empire, it is reasonable that guinea pigs were raised nearby. There is no hint whatsoever that this space functioned as an "observatory" in which people looked out at the sun. It seems to have a place for the sun to enter the dark cave of the underworld under the wings of the condor.

A noteworthy feature of the Temple of the Condor is a fountain in the structure containing the guinea pig hutches, which can only be accessed through the temple. Flowing water played an important role in Andean culture, animating sacred spaces through the process of *camay*. The stone-lined channel feeding the Stairway of the Fountains is diverted away from the top of the stairway to the northern wall of the Torreon, forming two fountains. The presence of water and fountains may have been important for animating the Torreon. Likewise, the fountain near the Temple of the Condor may signify its ritual importance and sacred meaning. The two doorways into the Temple of the Condor have double jambs, further indicating the sacred nature of the space.

Intimachay

In 1984, Dearborn, Schreiber, and White (1987) described an unusual cave with a light tube pointing toward sunrise on December solstice, which they named Intimachay, or Cave of the Sun, and suggested it functioned as an observatory. The light tube is formed by an L-shaped groove cut in the bedrock, which is 7 feet long. The north side and top are constructed of irregular masonry. The resulting tube is eighteen inches wide, and halfway along the north side there is an opening to the tube through which ceremonial objects may have been placed to receive sunlight on the mornings of December solstice, called *Capac Raymi.*

The cave does not have the careful and elegant stonework of those of Llaco, Kenko Grande near Cusco, the Temple of the Moon, or the Royal Mausoleum. When measured by Dearborn and colleagues, the view outward through the tube provided a view of an approximately two-degree long stretch of the horizon near the sunrise point at December solstice. The area immediately behind the tube is very cramped and is an unlikely place for ceremonial viewing of sunrise.

Just behind the opening is an overhanging natural rock, which blocks the view of most of the horizon from anyone in the central part of the cave. A small section of the overhanging rock may have been intentionally worked in order to allow a view of a very small section of the horizon from the interior of the cave. On the basis of their measurements, Dearborn, Schreiber, and White claim that the first gleam of the sun at December solstice would have appeared in the window approximately three minutes of arc away from the lowest part of the triangular viewing area. The first gleam would have been visible for only a few days before and after solstice. This remarkable accuracy has not been confirmed by the recent measurements of Ziólkowski, et al. (2013).

What does this apparent attempt to align a portion of the light tube so remarkably close to the rising point of the sun signify? The Inca were certainly able to establish very precise angles in working stone, and the orientation of the light tube could have been established relatively easily by observing the position of the first gleam. It seems unnecessarily precise. Because the horizon is irregular at that location, an experienced observer could identify the date of solstice by watching the rising position on the horizon. Perhaps it was intended to be a training device for novice sun watchers to identify the point on the horizon where they should be looking for the first gleam of sunrise?

The cave is clearly not intended for public ceremonies such as could have occurred at June solstice at the Sacred Plaza. The most careful stonework is in the two sides of the light tube cut out of granite and perhaps that portion of Intimachay is the most ceremonially important. Objects to be illuminated by the sun and thereby animated or empowered by the luminous action of *camay* could have been inserted into the light tube through the side opening.

The Temple of the Mortars

The Temple of the Mortars is approached through a double-jamb doorway on the south side of the group of structures. The floor contains two shallow basins carved out of bedrock. It is not clear how much rock was excavated to leave the two mortars above ground level. It is one of the few structures whose interior windows frame both Wayna Picchu and Machu Picchu Peak. If the stone to build most of Machu Picchu came from the western quarry, the Temple of the Mortars must have been one of the earliest to be constructed in the Eastern Sector.

The building probably was not roofed, suggesting the importance of sunlight touching the rock and water of the mortars. It is a potentially powerful combination for animating the

The Temple of the Mortars. Steven Bein photo.

huaca through *camay*. The mortars may have been the location for the reenactment of a major mytho-historic event in the founding of the Inca Empire. Zuidema (1982) discusses the myth recounted by the chronicler Molina of the sun god rising out of a spring called Susurpuquio.

The story recounts the eve of the pivotal battle of the Inca Empire, when Cusco was attacked by the *Chancas.* Pachacuti's father, Inca Viracocha, and his brother, Urco, had fled the town. Pachacuti remained to defend the city. On the eve of the battle, Pachacuti visited the spring called Susurpuquio and watched a flat crystal mirror fall into the water. A man rose up from the water adorned with serpents and puma skins. His head was crowned with three rays, like the sun. He said, "Come here, my son, don't be afraid, for I am the Sun. Your father and I know that you will conquer many nations." (Zuidema 1982:216)

The myth continues that after the Sun disappeared, the crystal mirror remained behind in the spring. Pachacuti took it, and in it he saw all the things he wanted. In the ensuing battle, the *Chancas* were severely defeated. Even the stones rose up to fight on Pachacuti's side. If Pachacuti built Machu Picchu, it does not seem too unlikely that he would have performed ceremonial reenactments of this pivotal event of the Inca Empire. Zuidema suggests that the myth refers to the sun of the month of June solstice and the emergence of the sun from water.

The northern mortar receives sunlight from the single eastern window on the morning of equinox and the southern mortar on the morning of June solstice (Gullberg 2010). While the shaft of sunlight at equinox covers the mortar, the light that reaches the southern mortar covers only a portion. Arthur Kaufmann (Malville, personal communication) has extensively studied the light patterns in the Temple of the Mortars. He suggests that afternoon light entering the temple causes distinct patterns of light on the eastern wall on the afternoons of all the important solar calendrical events: the zenith sun, anti-zenith sun, summer solstice, and winter solstice.

The Petroglyph at the Unfinished Temple

Like many Inca sites, Machu Picchu was undergoing continuing construction and modification at the time of abandonment. One area in the process of development hosts an unusual circular diagram carved on a flat piece of original, in situ granite. This unique rock carving may represent a visual diagram for a *ceques* system. Every major Inca settlement probably had a system (Zuidema 1964). We suggest that Machu Picchu had one as well. A study of the rock carving comparing map topographical features and visual sightlines from the Unfinished Temple establishes lines to several important objects, and equinox and solstice azimuths.

Writing in 1653, Jesuit scholar Bernabe Cobo described the system azimuths of 41 *ceques* and 328 *huacas* that surround the Sun Temple (Cobo 1983). The *huacas* consisted of natural features such as springs, unusual rocks, and caves, as well as artificial structures such as elaborately carved rocks, fountains, pools, and temples (Bauer 1998; Zuidema 1964). Tom Zuidema

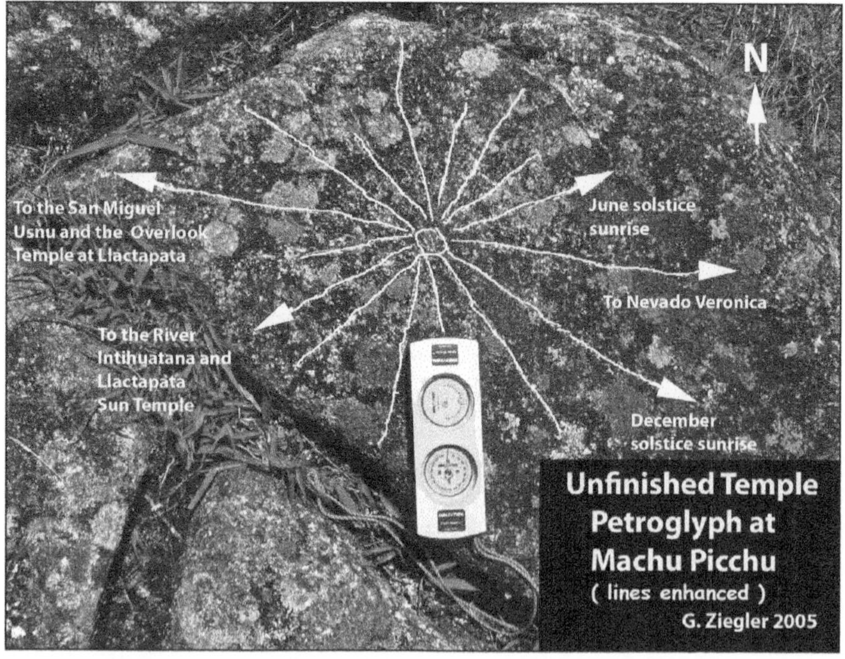

proposes that the 328 *huacas* represented successive days of the sidereal lunar calendar, and that the flow of time in the Inca world was marked by worship rituals at consecutive *huacas* by kinship groups.

In addition to markers of calendrical time, Zuidema suggests that *ceques* might have been sightlines to sacred mountains and astronomical phenomena, as well as geometrical partitions that organized the sacred landscape. If a defining characteristic of a *ceque* involves a line of shrines and sacred buildings that have geographical, astronomical, or cosmological meaning, then the linear groups associated with and at Machu Picchu may qualify.

Urubamba Intihuatana

We have since explored much of the surrounding region along the Urubamba River down to the old Inca bridge site, Chuquichaca, the high county to the north above the

G. Ziegler photo.

Lucumayu drainage, and the upper Aobamba Canyon to the *tambo* site of Palcay. The result is much useful data. We surveyed a particularly interesting shrine group reported by Bingham, which is centered on a large shaped stone and water features beside the river, called the Urubamba *Intihuatana.* It lies on the equinox line between Cerro Machu Picchu and the Overlook Temple at Llactapata (Bingham 2002; Malville, Thomson, and Ziegler 2004).

This must have been by Inca design. *Ceques* have many interpretations, one of which is visual alignments to sacred objects. This riverside *huaca* is a compelling example. It contains many features used to describe *ceques* at Cusco. It has sightlines, water channels, a spring and fountain, a cave, basins aligned east-west to the Overlook Temple, and a nearby structure that may have housed resident ritual specialists.

The large shaped granite rock contains a leveled platform that provides views of the Overlook Temple on the Llactapata ridge and the *Intihuatana* stone of Machu Picchu. The location

G. Ziegler measuring azimuths at the *Intihuatana*. Paolo Greer photo.

is critical for its view. If it was located a few feet to the south, the view of the Overlook Temple would be blocked by canyon walls. Machu Picchu's pyramid and *Intihuatana usnu* above the Sacred Plaza are clearly visible with the base of the carved stone oriented in this direction.[20]

The site's primary feature is the *intihuatana*, a somewhat worn, but finely carved stone situated at the group's western boundary. Its dimensions overall are 14 feet along the flat northern face by 10.5 feet wide. The tiers get increasingly smaller as they rise and are adjoined on the southwest corner by a set of steps too small to serve any necessary function. There appears at present to be three steps, but the stone has been subject to enough erosion to make the original number uncertain. The top of the northern face is flat and includes remains of what was perhaps a gnomon. The lines of the river *intihuatana* were rotated from the site's predominant east-west orientations to point in the direction of Machu Picchu's *Intihuatana,* about 44 degrees. The line of sight is clear be-

Reflection basins. Paolo Greer photo.

tween the two *intihuatanas* and they may easily have been viewed from one another.

When filled with water, two nearby carved basins provide double reflections of the Overlook Temple; they also would have provided reflections of the setting sun near the date of equinox. It is possible that the river *intihuatana* is part of a *ceque* line that connects the Machu Picchu *Intihuatana* to the Overlook Temple. From the Overlook Temple, there is a north-south line that goes directly to the highest and most southern group at Llactapata. One of the more intriguing areas found on the river *intihuatana* site is a complex incorporating several common *huaca* motifs, a fountain, the two basins, and a cave.

The fountain structure is situated upslope from the *intihuatana.* The face of the fountain is oriented on a 090/270-degree axis and was designed to receive water from the east into a channel. A ledge was carved near the base of the fountain

G. Ziegler photo.

Paolo Greer photo.

and worn examples of seats or shelves remain sculpted to the west. The channel was engineered to distribute water to each of the four outlets on the fountain's face. Within the channel, a small baffle was constructed at each outlet to ensure an even diversion of water flow through that opening. The fountain is now dry, but would have once been fed by an upslope spring.

Unfortunately, the historical record provides no guidance as to whether these various linear groupings of shrines in the Llactapata–Machu Picchu neighborhood have a meaning and function similar to those of the *ceques.* We suggest they do.

Notes

17. It seems unusual that the *cancha* identified as the Royal Residence lacks the status-significant double-jamb entranceway. Although a distance across the big lower plaza from the Torreon and water system, the main hilltop *cancha* to the north with the important double-jamb feature could have served as such. If so, how would the urban design model of *hanan* and *hurin* fit with this? Pachacuti was of the *hanan* group in Cusco. The less impressive and lower north-side half of Machu Picchu is thought to represent *hurin.*

18. Project workers with the Instituto Nacional de Cultura (INC) reconstructed what is called the House of Three Windows just below the summit on the west facing side of Huayna Picchu before our project at Llactapata. They called it a *colca*, or storehouse. However, as the only building placed upon Machu Picchu's most important geological feature, it is unlikely that it was intended for storage. The direct perpendicular alignment with the main sectors at Llactapata is significant. A shaped-stone replication of what appears to be the Llactapata ridge gives a special visual association. We believe it to be one of the spiritually important *huacas.*

19. Bauer and Dearborn have severely criticized Zuidema for the lack of any evidence for attention to the anti-zenith sun in the archaeological record.

20. The riverside *huaca* sets on a steep slope a hundred yards or so below the railroad and near the hydroelectric plant, which is now the end of the line for the tracks. A local family told us that they have owned the land for many years. When the grandfather moved there, the shaped stone had a vertical protrusion like the *intihuatana* at Machu Picchu, explaining why it was called the Urubamba *Intihuatana* by Bingham. They say that it was knocked off during a slide created by construction workers when the plant was being built. Unfortunately, with the exception of major sites, destruction with little regard for archaeological history continues, as new roads are bulldozed through ruins and walls dismantled for building stone.

Seven
The Llactapata Ceremonial Complex—Machu Picchu's Observatory and Sun Temple

We have previously discussed some of Llactapata's unique relationship with Machu Picchu. Located less than three miles away, but several hours travel time during Inca occupation, Llactapata was a busy complex of separated, interconnected groups, ceremonial features, temples, *usnus,* a water-focused sector, and a large urban agricultural district supporting Pachacuti's royal estate. The exploration of the steep, dense, cloud forest slopes, subsequent location and survey of lost ruins, and discovery of the Inca trail connecting Machu Picchu's Hanging Bridge by our team during 2003–2004 is an interesting story. This chapter is an edited and shortened version of the original field report titled "El Observatorio de Machu Picchu: Redescubrimiento de Llactapata y su templo solar," published in Peru's professional journal, *Revista Andean,* in Spanish (Malville, Thomson, and Ziegler 2004).

Despite its relative proximity to Machu Picchu, Llactapata is a site that had not been investigated since its first reporting by Hiram Bingham in 1912. In May 2003, a thorough survey of the site was made by a research group led by Hugh Thomson and Gary Ziegler, including Kim Malville, John Leivers, Amy Finger, and a determined, talented field team. The expedition, generously supported by the Royal Geographical Society of London, made a systematic exploration of the ridge and

G. Ziegler photo.

mountain slope of Llactapata, which lies on the western side of the Aobamba drainage facing Machu Picchu.

A primary objective was to find and study Hiram Bingham's Llactapata group, which had not been located since his initial reporting of the site in 1913. We planned a thorough investigation to discover other sectors of the site that had not been reported. Finally, we intended to survey and map for the first time the full extent of the extended Llactapata site with detailed plans of each sector and interpret the relationship of Llactapata to Machu Picchu given recent archaeo-astronomical work at Machu Picchu. Our fieldwork established that the size and importance of Llactapata had been greatly underestimated and that its alignment and relationship to Machu Picchu is central to any interpretation of the site.

History

The first published account of Llactapata was by Hiram Bingham as part of his article on Machu Picchu "In the Wonderland of Peru" for *National Geographic* (Bingham 1913). While the clearance and excavation of Machu Picchu was taking place in 1912, Bingham had sent various reconnaissance teams into the surrounding area to look for further Inca sites.

A team led by his assistant Kenneth Heald attempted to head up the Aobamba Valley, but met with "almost insuperable difficulty," as "the jungle was so dense as to be almost impassable. There was no trail and the trees were so large and the foliage so dense that observations were impossible even after the trail had been cut." Heald's team was further discouraged when an *arriero* was almost bitten by a poisonous snake.

Bingham himself then attempted to investigate the area and in his own words "got into the reaches of the valley about ten days later and found some interesting ruins ... The end of that day found us on top of a ridge between the valleys of the Aobamba and the Salcantay." Here Bingham reported a site called "Llactapata, the ruins of an Inca castle ... We found evidence that some Inca chieftain had built his castle here and had included in the plan ten or a dozen buildings."

After mapping and photographing the site, Bingham pressed on rapidly up the valley to the site of Palcay, which lies at the head of the Aobamba Valley. He had spent just five daylight hours at Llactapata. Unfortunately, he left few published details for anyone who might want to return to the site. Both the map published with the 1913 magazine article and his account are imprecise: "The end of that day found us on top of a ridge between the valleys of the Aobamba and the Salcantay" gives little indication of where exactly he was between two long and densely covered valleys.

The same difficult vegetation that had defeated Bingham's assistant Heald still characterizes the area, and without proper compass bearings or directions, no further expeditions reported on it. Nor did they have much inclination to do so. Bingham's decidedly halfhearted and incomplete account of it would have given them little incentive.

It is worth noting that one reason this region so close to Machu Picchu had been relatively ignored is that the Inca architecture does not appear as impressive as that of Machu Picchu and the upper Urubamba region. Machu Picchu is constructed from local fine-grained, white granite, while most Vilcabamba sites to the west were built from a fragile, metamorphic material that could not be shaped polygonally or easily rounded. The result is a rather crude-appearing, coursed construction consisting of flat slabs and blocks joined with mortar.

However, the evidence shows that walls were coated inside and out with a light-colored clay, hiding the stonework beneath a smooth, attractive coating. This was first mentioned by Ziegler (1999) at the Vilcabamba site, Choquequirao, as a possible reason why this major Inca complex may not have been given its proper importance by investigators.

Over the years, Thomson, Ziegler, and others had passed by the vegetation-covered ruins that they assumed was Bingham's insignificant Llactapata. Then, in 2002, Thomson researched the unpublished journals of Hiram Bingham at the Sterling Memorial Library at Yale University, and the collection of unpublished photographs at the Peabody Museum. He found that Bingham had left a more detailed record of his investigations at Llactapata than had been published. Comparing field notes, Thompson and Ziegler realized that the structures they had each visited did not in any way resemble the group of structures diagramed and described by Bingham. What really was hidden in the dense cloud forest so close to Machu Picchu yet to be discovered and revealed? Where and what was Llactapata?

Armed with new clues from the Yale archives and the prospect of another exciting adventure, we set out to organize the next expedition. A first step was obtaining the required official investigation permit from the National Institute of Culture (INC). The Director of the INC Cusco department, anthropologist David Ugarte, soon acquired proper authorization for us. We were given permission to conduct surface investigations but not to excavate or collect cultural material. Peru was still smarting from allowing Yale to cart away the Machu Picchu collection.

Amy Finger photo.

Discovery and Investigation

Supported by the Royal Geographical Society and John Hemming, former Director of the RGS and author of the definitive book, *The Conquest of the Incas,* our well-equipped and funded expedition team arrived in Cusco in April 2003. It was truly a flashback to Hiram Bingham's day of the big expeditions. We had several crews of specialists and helpers, a railroad car full of provisions, Chilean wines, and a Cessna 208 on-call for aerial reconnaissance.

Our Cusco-based logistic coordinators, British Consul Barry Walker and Peru resident-journalist-explorer Nick Asheshov, even managed a private train for us down to the end of the line below Machu Picchu. An old companion of previous explorations, Pio Espinosa, met us at the railhead with a string of pack horses and a crew of local Quechua-speaking wranglers. Eventually, a small mountain of provisions was moved up to a campsite high on the ridge above. The explorations began.

Compiling data each night from the day's exploration in the big dining tent that served for meals, happy hour, and as

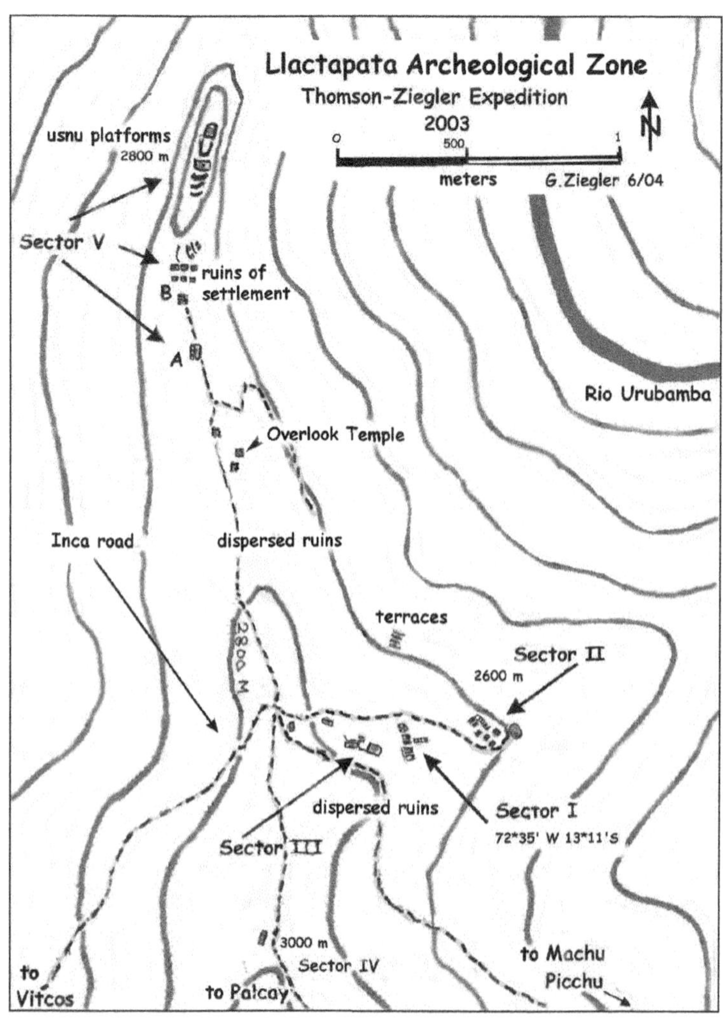

expedition headquarters, we were able to gradually piece together the expanse and importance of the site.

The archaeological zone when finally explored, surveyed, and mapped, consists of several interrelated high-status building groups, agricultural areas, isolated structures, lower-status urban ruins, and a connecting road network scattered over several square miles. The zone has different sectors that we surveyed and diagrammed on individual site plans. A number of isolated structures and features are indicated as scattered or assorted ruins on the general site map. Some site plans are less detailed, indicating that additional field information was needed. We undertook additional investigations in 2004 and 2005, bringing in local archaeologists and specialists to help with interpretation.

The area that we designate as the Llactapata Archaeological Zone is approximately two miles long by one mile wide, containing more than one hundred-thirty manmade structures and features, which we have organized into five sectors.

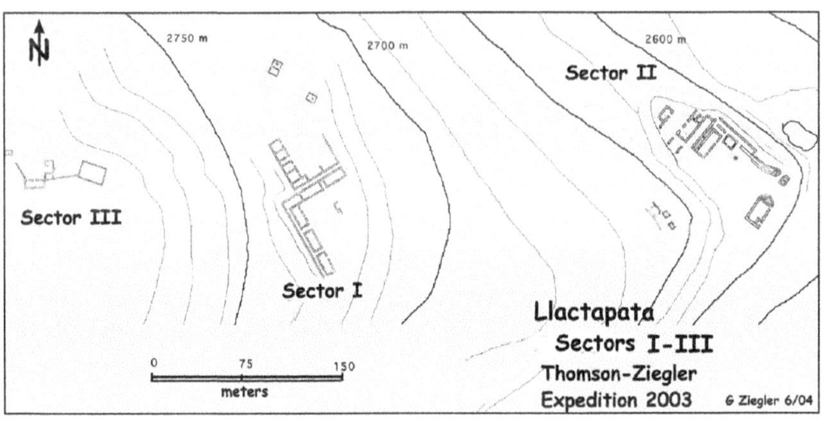

Llactapata Sectors 1-3 site map. G. Ziegler diagram.

The central part of the zone lies some 2 miles from Machu Picchu. The three central groups, Sectors I–III, are situated on a direct east-west line along an easterly running ridge that descends from the Salcantay highlands above. The groups form an area approximately 650 yards long by 175 yards wide, extending downward from an elevation of 9,000 feet to 8,500 feet. The two upper groups, Sectors I and III, are 150 yards apart, with Sector I some 100 feet lower in elevation. The lower Sector II is 270 yards distance down the slope at an elevation ranging from 8,600 to 8,500 feet. Sectors IV and the largest sector, V, are roughly 1,000 yards distant. More features undoubtedly remain to be located between those sectors now surveyed and identified.

Sector I: Bingham's Llactapata Rediscovered

Here is Hugh Thomson's description of the exciting find: "Gary and I checked it against Bingham's original map. At first the two didn't seem to match. Then I spotted a tiny detail I had never noticed before, partly because I had never been looking for it—a tiny nubbin on the entrance to one passageway indicating that it was a double-jamb doorway. Suspecting that it might be the one Bob had first come across, we realigned the maps so that the doorways lay on top of one another. It was a perfect fit. We were without question standing in the middle of the Llactapata that Bingham had reported ninety years ago and which had been missing ever since."

Revelation followed revelation. Following a long sunken passageway that ran some 150 yards, we emerged onto a plateau that faced directly onto Machu Picchu. The sightline to the great city was remarkable, directly over the various valleys in between. Nor was it accidental: Dr. Kim Malville, the scholar of Inca astronomy who accompanied us, calculated that it lay directly in line with sunrise at the June solstice and with the rise of the Pleiades constellation that was used in the Andes from time immemorial to tell the beginning of certain agricultural seasons. The Incas had built Llactapata as a place from which they could both admire Machu Picchu and use it to take astronomical readings. The layout of the main buildings also corresponded with the layout used at the Coricancha, the main Sun Temple in Cuzco.

The Sun Temple

Sector I consists of a complex set of seven buildings, passageways, and courtyards, some of which are remarkably similar in scale and orientation to the Coricancha. The Inca road that starts at the so-called "drawbridge" or "hanging bridge" at Machu Picchu provided an elaborate ritual entrance to Llactapata.

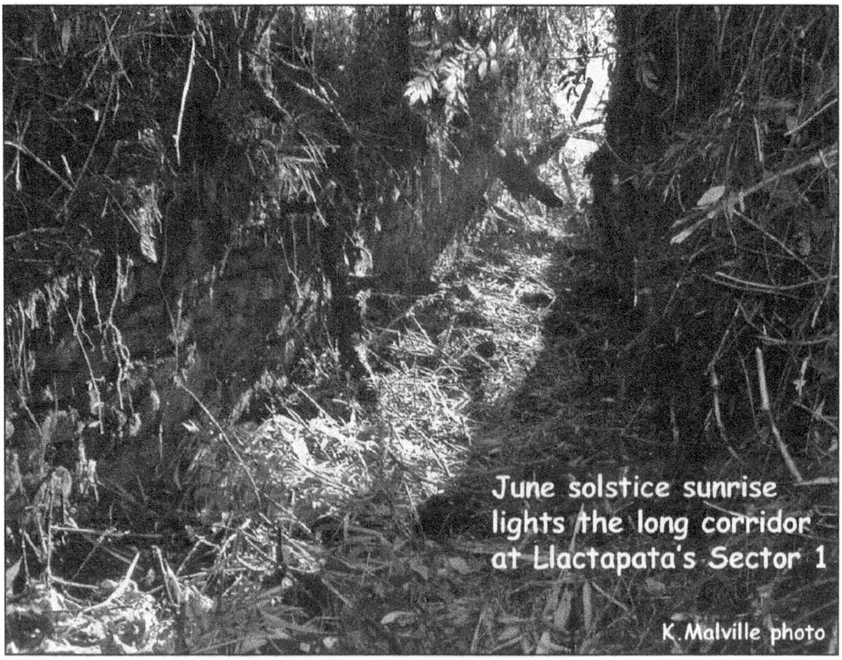
June solstice sunrise
lights the long corridor
at Llactapata's Sector 1
K.Malville photo

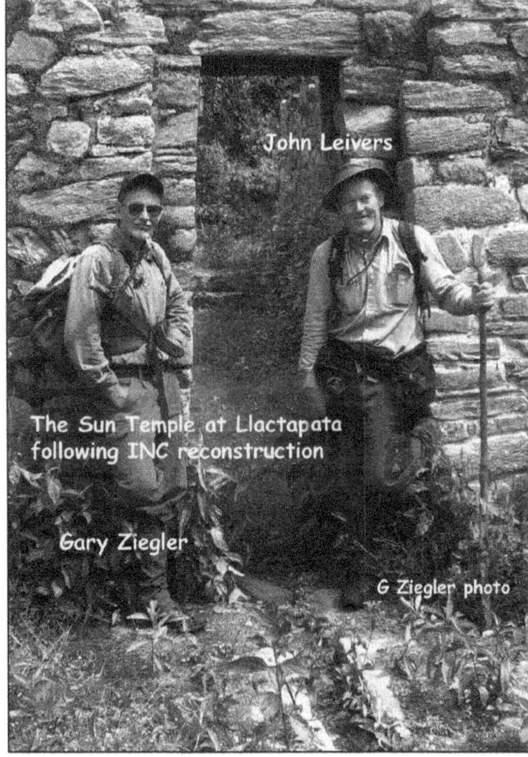

John Leivers
The Sun Temple at Llactapata
following INC reconstruction
Gary Ziegler
G Ziegler photo

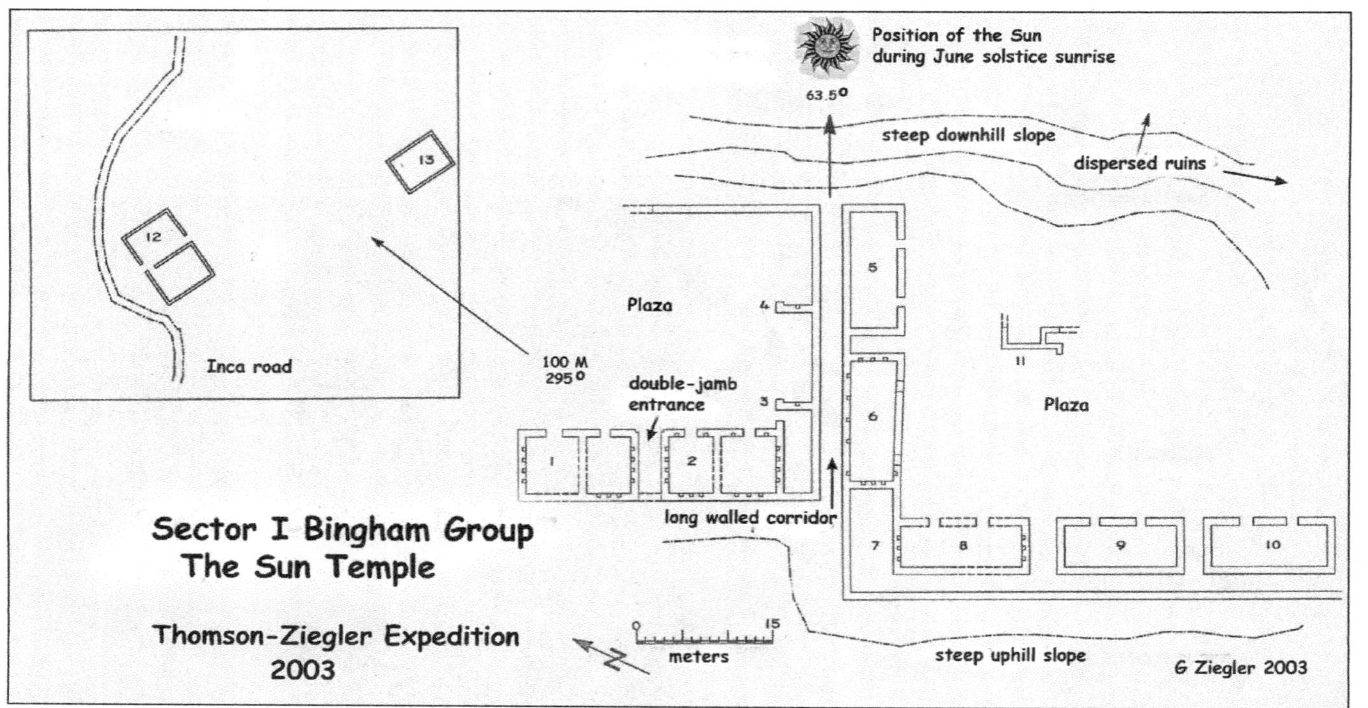

Llactapata site plan, Sector I. G. Ziegler diagram.

It would have allowed the Inca and his retinue to visit Llactapata on special occasions to celebrate the rising of the sun at June solstice and the heliacal rising of the Pleiades some twelve to fifteen days before solstice. The group extends some 100 yards along the hillside and contains seven buildings, two courtyards, and two ceremonial corridors. The corridors open to an azimuth of approximately 63.5 degrees on the northeastern horizon and provide views of the rising sun on June solstice, the rising of the Pleiades, and Machu Picchu itself.

Front of the Llactapata Sun Temple that faces Machu Picchu, after INC reconstruction. Carlos Aranibar photo.

The longer corridor, which measures 2 yards wide and 36 yards long, has no side doors or side passages, implying its function as a ceremonial passageway. The precise center of the corridor is difficult to establish because of irregular walls, but its length frames a window of approximately 4 degrees along the horizon. On the 6-degree elevated horizon, the first gleam of sunrise on June solstice has an azimuth of 64.2 degrees. The Pleiades star cluster covers approximately 1 degree on the sky, and in 1500 CE it rose close to the center of the horizon window, at an azimuth of approximately 66 degrees. On June solstice the Pleiades was a harbinger of sunrise, appearing on the horizon perhaps fifteen minutes ahead of the sun.

The short corridor that opens onto the northern courtyard contains a double-jam doorway, characteristic of a high-status or ceremonially important structure. Since Llactapata was unknown to the Spanish conquerors, the historical record provides no guidance as to the function of this site, but the similarities in orientation, design, and scale to the Coricancha are suggestive of its ritual significance.

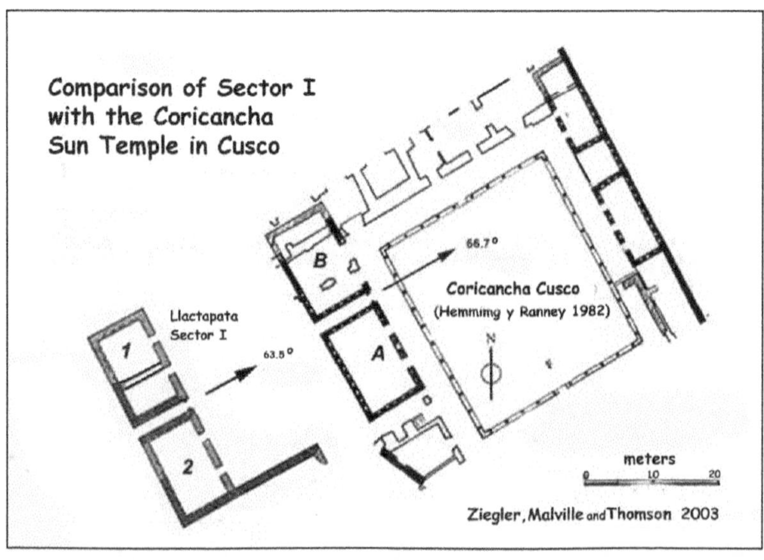

The Coricancha of Cusco is the great exemplar of sun temples of the Inca. It contained seven halls, six of which opened onto a courtyard, some 38 yards on a side. These buildings were dedicated to various deities such as the sun, moon, Venus, the Pleiades, thunder, and rainbow. The western section of the courtyard consisted of a continuous façade containing two halls surrounding a passage with a double-jamb doorway. As the most important sanctuary in the Inca Empire, it served as a model for other temples of the sun throughout the empire. The most important shrines of the Coricancha appear to have been dedicated to the sun and the moon.

Although the Spanish destroyed much of the Coricancha, early colonial chroniclers had extensively described its buildings and rituals. Table I compares features of Llactapata's Sector I with those of the Coricancha. The opening to the horizon, established by the western end of the corridor and room D, is approximately 5.6 degrees wide. The rising position of the Pleiades was also close to the center of that horizon window, while the June solstice sun rose to the north. The center of the courtyard of the Coricancha may have contained a basin symbolic of water out of which both the sun and the Pleiades were born.

At Llactapata, the courtyard contains two U-shaped shrines with niches that face the June solstice sunrise and the Pleiades.

Table 1 - Comparison of Sector I at Llactapata and the Coricancha

Feature	Llactapata	Coricancha
Corridor behind double-jamb doorway	9x2 yards	10x1 yards
Halls on either side of corridor	12x4 yards	14x8 yards
Total N-S Length	98 yards	74 yards
Orientation of corridor	63.5 degrees	66.7 degrees
Elevation of northeast horizon	6 degrees	5.6 degrees
Courtyard beyond corridor	32x29 yards	39x37 yards
Niches in hall south of corridor	18	25
Total number of halls	7	7

Water symbolism may have been important in both places. Zuidema (1982) suggests that the spring of Susumarca, to the northeast of Cusco, may have been the mythological spring (Susurpuquio) out of which an image of the sun appeared to Pachacuti. A spring and water shrine (Sector II) lies some 275 yards to the east of the Llactapata sun temple.

The sun temple at Llactapata is not alone in the Inca realm to be modeled after the Coricancha—it apparently served as a model for other sun temples, such as those at Quito, Pachacamac, Vitcos, Willka Waman, Huánuco Pampa, and the Island of the Sun.

The architecture and dramatic landscape of Machu Picchu suggest that it was a place with considerable depth of meaning and sacred power. Lying at the entrance to the Vilcabamba, Llactapata adds to the significance of Machu Picchu by extending the size and complexity of its ritual neighborhood. The presence of a structure so similar to the Coricancha at Llactapata rather than at Machu Picchu is intriguing. The Inca emperor Pachacuti had substantial connections with the Coricancha, where he may have been crowned, to Machu Picchu, which he may have built, and the Vilcabamba, which he conquered. The ceremonial complex of Machu Picchu and Llactapata, interconnected by road and sightlines, may have been viewed as homologous to Cuzco and its sacred neighborhood. A further significance of the sun temple at Llactapata would have been that the June solstice sun rose over Machu Picchu.

Llactapata may also have been important because it provided a horizon calendar. Of great interest would have been the heliacal rising of the Pleiades near June 6–9, which may have been the first day of the Inca year (Zuidema 1982). The jagged horizon visible from Llactapata would have allowed precise tracking of the sun and determinations of the number of days before the heliacal rising of the Pleiades and the June solstice. In contrast to the irregular horizon of Llactapata, the smooth horizon at Cusco does not provide natural fiducial marks so pillars were erected by the Inca to mark the sunrise/

sunset positions at solstices and other significant dates (Bauer and Dearborn 1995; Rowe 1994; Zuidema 1982). The chroniclers noted the presence of the Cusco pillars, but their exact location is now a matter of some controversy among scholars.

Sector II

The group was visited and reported for the first time by David Drew and Hugh Thomson in 1982, who then mistakenly believed that they had relocated Bingham's lost Llactapata. It is indeed part of Llactapata, but not the group that Bingham found and reported (Thomson 2001). The sector consists of a tightly grouped assortment of carefully constructed large buildings, walls, and smaller structures arranged around a central plaza with several outlying structures of lesser quality.

The group sits upon a flat bench with a steep, rising embankment behind and a steep downhill slope to the front. Another leveled plaza-like area is situated just below (northeast), which may have been a pond or water feature, now dry and filled in. The only present water source identified for the region, a spring, is located just above to the south of the plaza and remains of a stone-lined water channel (*acequia*) originating at the spring are indicated on the site plan. This leads into a nicely constructed sunken, stone-lined enclosure resembling one of the fountains or ritual baths at Machu Picchu or Wiñay Wayna.

The main buildings (1–7) have shaped corner blocks of quartzite and coursed-slabs, with blocks for the walls. Remains of clay indicate that the structures were plastered. Roots and trees have crumbled parts of most structures, but some walls are standing close to their original height. Building 6 has a back wall height of 14 feet. Buildings 1, 2, and 6 had gabled roofs; building 12 may have as well. This is undetermined for the remainder. Buildings 1–7 had internal niches and some windows. Minor details are lacking because of the surveying demands created by the unexpected size and extent of the findings and lack of time.

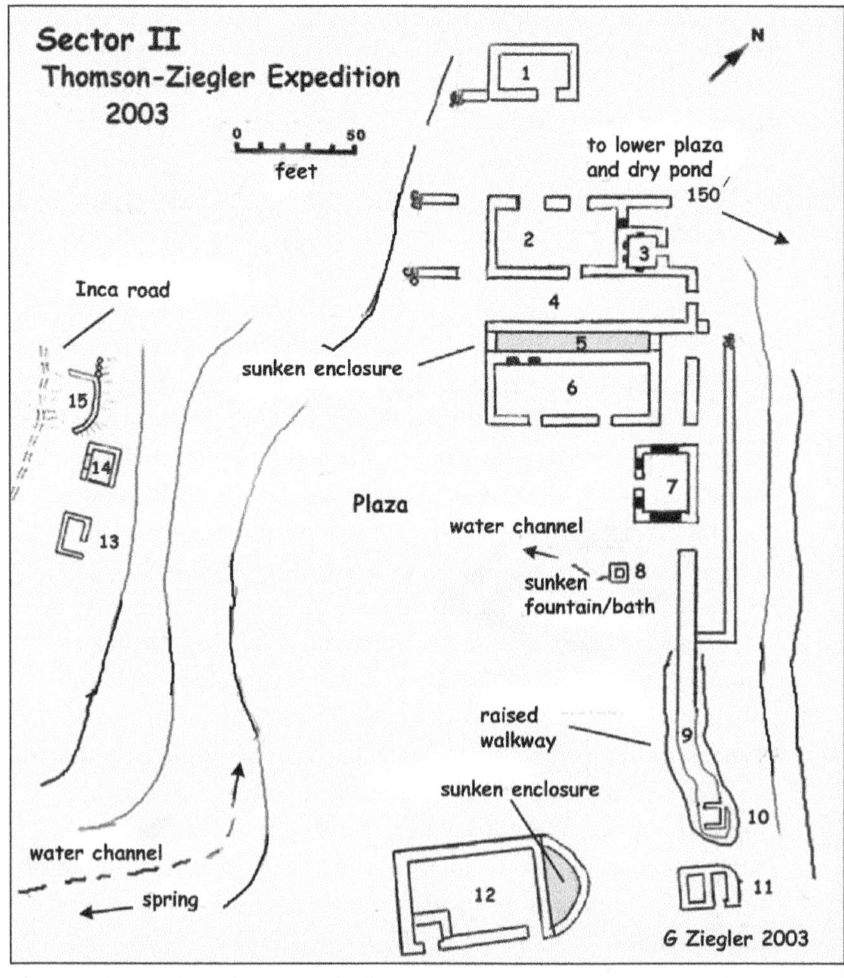

Llactapata Sector II site plan. G. Ziegler diagram.

By contrast, buildings 12–14 are of poorly constructed mortared fieldstone without niches. Building 13 has a low-walled open side and a long low window lined with adobe blocks. Four rocker-shaped grinding stones for corn were found inside, made of granite. Building 12 appears to have been modified by an internal enclosure. It is likely that local farmers or herders used these buildings in later times. Building 12 could have served as a caretaker residence or entrance control for the main group as suggested for building 12 in Sector I.

The central section of the group has multiple passageways that open out to a long, filled, low-walled platform/walkway that forms an overlook of Huayna Picchu, Machu Picchu, and the Veronica Range beyond. The long axis points to and views the Overlook Temple (Sector V).

Building 2 has a window that opens into a short corridor viewing Huayna Picchu. Building 3 is a small structure measuring 10x10 feet with four internal niches. The one entranceway faces 50 degrees toward Huayna Picchu. Its size and location suggest that it was a *huaca* (shrine).

Feature 4 is a courtyard-like area between building 2 and a long, sunken enclosure, or *recinto.* It is closed by a wall at the end that faces Huayna Picchu. Here an entranceway with an alignment of 50 degrees opens to the outside platform/walkway.

Structure 9 is a low wall slightly above the plaza level that measures 6 feet high on the downhill side. The wall merges into a raised earth platform, which takes a curious jog to terminate at building 10. The wall and mount may have been used as a ritual walkway to reach a shrine. This feature is a small 10x10-foot U-shaped structure (*masma*) with the open side facing inward to the plaza at 230 degrees.

Building 7 is an interesting feature. It is an unusual structure measuring 30x30 feet with internal niches and a single entranceway facing onto the plaza. The back, or Huayna Picchu side, lacks windows and has five rectangular niches. The two sides perpendicular to the entrance have matching long windows. The workmanship is in the best Vilcabamba style, with shaped corner blocks and carefully fitted, coursed wall stones. The location gives immediate access to the bath/fountain and water system. The building remains an enigma deserving further study.

A steep escarpment falls off to the northeast. Some 20 yards below is a sizable flat area (*pampa*), with swampy depressions and a profusion of water plants. We believe this was a pond and developed water feature associated with the group above. It was used as a base camp by both Bingham and our expedition.

Ramiro Abendanio
Examining structure
8, a bath or fountain at
Llactapata Sector 2
G Ziegler photo

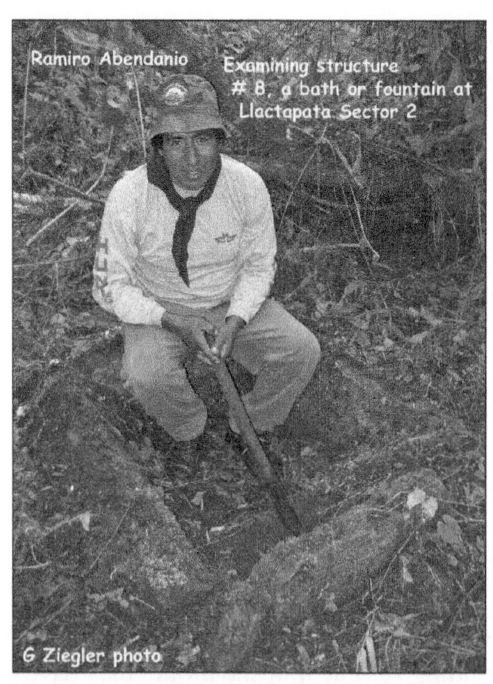

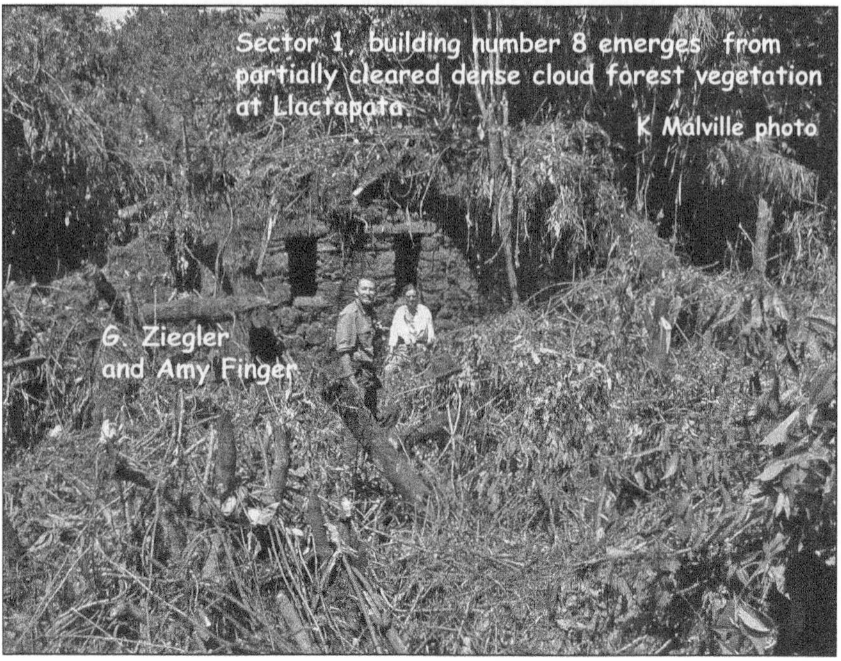
Sector 1, building number 8 emerges from
partially cleared dense cloud forest vegetation
at Llactapata.
K Malville photo
G. Ziegler
and Amy Finger

A most notable aspect of this sector is that the main group is orientated to face Huayna Picchu at an azimuth of 50 degrees, and the Overlook Temple at 320 degrees. This creates a sightline to each at a right angle, or 90 degrees to each other. The placement of the temple and/or Sector II had to be by design and carefully planned. Alignment on Huayna Picchu and its Three Windows shrine that looks back on the main sectors suggests that Huayna Picchu may have been an important spiritual focus of Sector II (Ziegler and Malville 2006).

Sector II has a number of unusual features that appear to have had a ceremonial function. The main group is orientated to face Huayna Picchu at an azimuth of 50 degrees. The long axis of the group points to the Overlook Temple at 320 degrees, similar to the long axis of Sector I. Near the summit of Huayna Picchu is the House of Three Windows, a shrine containing a replica stone closely resembling the Llactapata ridge that focuses attention on and is in alignment (230 degrees) with the Llactapata sites (Ziegler and Malville 2006).

A ritual fountain/bath along with a pond suggests that water was an important design element here as well. A small U-shaped shrine faces inward to the plaza and hillside. Its focus is directed toward the spring—the only water source for the area.

American anthropologist Susan Niles describes similar Inca sites as water shrines, or *moyas* (Niles 1999). Features at Sector II suggesting water ritual and *camay* include fountains, a canal leading from the only known water source in the area, a platform excavated from the hillside, and the evidence of an artificial lake.

Buildings 1, 2, and 6 could have served as temporary lodging for important parties traveling on official business, state sponsored pilgrimages, or ceremonial processions to and from Machu Picchu as a sort of high-status shrine and *tambo* with a ceremonial purpose. Like Wiñay Wayna on the eastern road to Machu Picchu, the main Llactapata groups are situated several hours travel along the western approach.

There are similarities between the two sites. Wiñay Wayna

is at an elevation of 8,530 feet and a distance of four miles from Machu Picchu. The Sector II group is at 8,850 feet elevation and about the same distance by the original western road. Both are designed around water features. Reinhard (2002) believes that Wiñay Wayna was built as a ritual stopping place along the road to Machu Picchu. The similarities with Sector II suggest that it may have in part served the same function.

Sector III: The Usnu Group

Located some 110 yards from the uphill side of Sector I and only 98 feet higher in elevation, this sector is associated with Sector I. Building 2 is long, with three entranceways facing east onto a small plaza. The roof was probably gabled but considerable breakdown has occurred. No windows are evident. It measures 90x20 feet with the back wall 9.5 feet high. The alignment is cardinal north-south. Buildings 3 and 4 border the north side of the plaza. Building 3 is low-walled with the slope falling off to the north and west, leaving a higher north-facing wall with an outside niche.

Building 4 is more interesting. Most of its wall stone is shaped white granite similar to that of Machu Picchu, making the architecture unique for the area. The material must have been imported from either near Machu Picchu or some closer isolated granite dike. A single internal niche faces east toward the one entrance. Sadly, this unique small structure, probably an important *huaca*, was destroyed in 2005 by looters, *huaqueros* looking for treasure. When we returned, only a deep pit and scattered stones remained.

A passageway leads down through a gateway between buildings 3 and 4 to feature 5, the most important structure of the group, which appears to be a sacred platform (*usnu*). The *usnu* is a 60x40-foot raised, earth-filled platform that is enclosed by a 5-foot high retaining wall. It is connected to building 4 by a 60-foot long low wall. Stone steps lead onto the platform from the northeast side. The platform is aligned 20 degrees by 110 degrees and overlooks Sector I below.

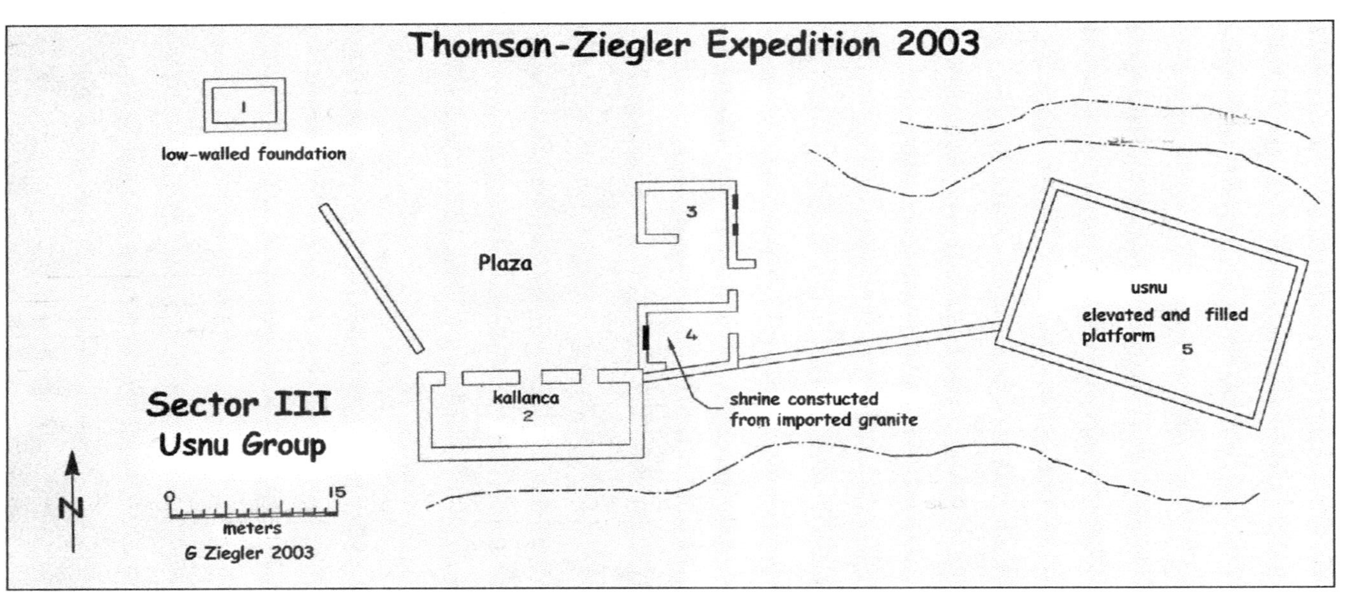

Llactapata Sector III site plan. G. Ziegler diagram.

Another low wall, 40 feet long, leads off from the northwest corner of building 2 at 330 degrees. Beyond the wall is a low-walled rectangular structure—building 1—that is similar in size and placement to outlying structures at other sections. It may have been built for a caretaker or attendant.

The main buildings and plaza are aligned with cardinal directions. Johan Reinhard (2002) has written of the importance to the Inca of cardinal directions, equinox alignments, and their unique relationship to sacred mountains at Machu Picchu. Although alignments would somewhat differ, it follows that this may be true for Llactapata sites as well. For example, the northwest wall of the plaza, aligned at 335 degrees, is in directional line to the Overlook Temple of Sector V. However, it was not possible to establish whether the temple can be seen from the plaza. A similar wall running out at an angle from a building at Cotacoca creates a sightline to the water shrine Pinchaunuyoc, near Choquequirao (Ziegler and Thomson 2002).

An important feature of any site is the large *usnu* platform. The term has several meanings. *Usnu* is used to describe a stepped platform upon which the Inca was seated from an early description by Guaman Poma (Poma 1956 [1613]). An *usnu* has also been described as a place to view sunset with markers on the horizon (Zuidema 1986). The great *usnu* of Cusco, *Usnu Capac,* had a central pillar for astronomical sighting (Moseley 1993). The name appropriately describes raised platforms associated with ceremonial sites.

With an alignment of 110 degrees and 20 degrees, the Sector III platform is orientated close to the December solstice line for the rising sun of 112 degrees for Machu Picchu, noted by Johan Reinhard (2002). As no significant summits are close to this alignment to suggest a topographic focus, nor does the platform align toward Machu Picchu, it is possible that the primary ritual activity is related to the December solstice. Overlook *miradores* and raised platforms are common throughout the region but few are of this large size. Only hilltop platforms at Choquequirao and Cerro San Miguel are larger (Lee 2000; Reinhard 2002; Ziegler 2001). The size suggests that this was a very important ceremonial location. Sector III requires additional study.

Sector IV: The Reinhard Group

During 1985, Johan Reinhard conducted an exploratory investigation of the upper regions of the Aobamba drainage. He visited the high site of Palcay (11,800 feet elevation) previously documented by Bingham (Bingham 1913). While descending down to the Urubamba Canyon, he surveyed and reported the building now identified as Sector IV (Reinhard 1990). Following his description and map, the site was re-located where indicated on a lofty shoulder of the Llactapata ridge at 9,800 feet elevation, among tall tree ferns.

The remaining walls are badly deteriorated. The main structure is a long, 120-foot narrow building with twelve entranceways spaced along the sides. No niches are visible. The building follows the slightly curved contour of a small hilltop. A number of equally spaced holes are centered along the inside floor. All have been opened by treasure hunters, or *huaqueros.* The holes appear to have been stone-lined chambers similar to others that have been observed in the Vilcabamba (Ziegler 2001, 2002). Three smaller low-walled rectangular structures are located nearby. The building is situated near the route of a likely Inca road that connected Palcay above with Llactapata and the main westward Inca road below.

Similar long structures with multiple entrances have been identified as meeting halls, such as the largest building at Machu Picchu, located outside and above the main gateway (Wright and Valencia 2001). These large buildings seem to be located near, or are part of, a larger site such as at Choquequirao, Cotacoca, and Machu Picchu. It would be unusual for a meeting hall to be placed as an isolated structure in a remote region. Some long buildings have been identified as storehouses. Examples are a group between the upper and lower

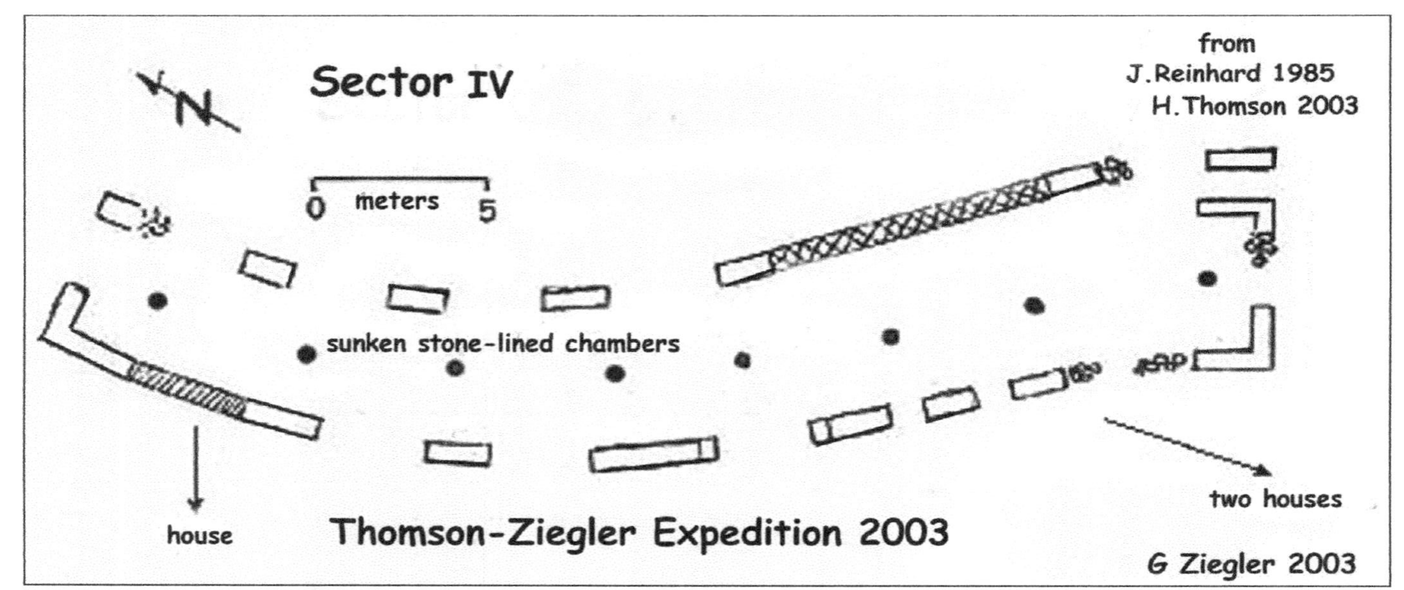

Llactapata Sector IV site plan. G. Ziegler diagram.

plazas at Choquequirao, and a long isolated building with multiple entrances and windows at Sapamarca (Ziegler 2001).

Storehouses were frequently placed in a high open area for ventilation, such as at Ollantaytambo (Protzen 1993). The holes or chambers in the floor present an enigma. Reinhard thought the holes were dug by *huaqueros.* However, several were now found to have visible stone linings. From excavations at Corihuayrachina, similar chambers were found to contain simple offerings and low-status burials (Ziegler 2002).

It is interesting that the alignment of the east wall of the Sector IV building is 40 degrees, creating a sightline to the summit of Huayna Picchu. An azimuth of 340 degrees for the opposite or north end offers a sightline down the Urubamba Canyon to the site of Sapamarca. The building may well have been a storehouse, located below the frost zone on the road to Palcay. Local residents may have used it as a convenient mausoleum at a later date, during or following the decline of Machu Picchu. The three low-walled structures may have been simple wood-sided huts for a caretaker family.

Sector V: Group A and Group B

This complicated sector encompasses a large area of the lower ridge dividing the Santa Teresa Valley and the Aobamba drainage, terminating when the two rivers merge in the Urubamba River and Canyon at an elevation of 4,900 feet. The ridge runs from 9,200 feet down to a partially clear saddle at 8,500 feet. From the saddle, the ridge rises steeply up into several rocky crags with steep cliffs on either side before again plunging downward. The upper portion is cloaked in heavy, dense forest and thick, nearly impenetrable vegetation.

A rough trail reaches the saddle from the Santa Teresa Valley side. A seasonal hut and several cornfields account for the cleared areas. Four main groups were located and incompletely surveyed: Groups (*conjuntos*) A and B, the Overlook Temple, and the crag top platforms (*usnus*). Several freshly dug holes indicated that the local farmer had visions of buried treasure.

The central feature is the solitary, unique two-story building perched on a ledge viewing Machu Picchu, first reported in 1982 and now described as the Overlook Temple.

Group A

This feature is a rectangularly walled compound (*cancha)* measuring 75x55 feet enclosing a long three-room, badly crumbling building. The outside wall is 6 feet high and 3 feet wide, consisting of crude slab construction. The alignment is cardinal with east-facing entranceways offering a sightline to Cerro Machu Picchu.

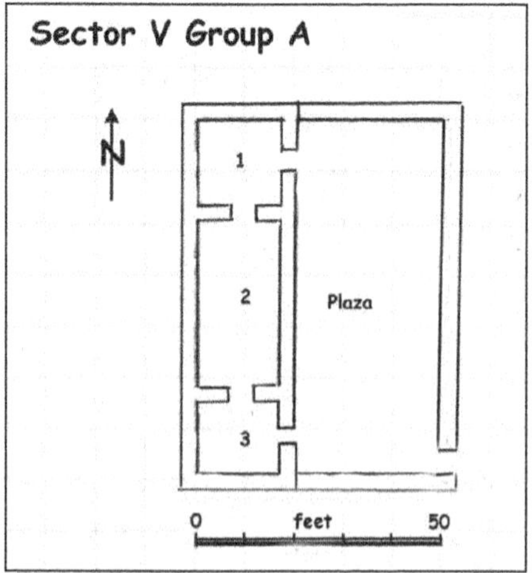

Llactapata Sector V-A site plan.
G. Ziegler diagram.

Group B

Located 200 yards down the ridge and at a slightly lower elevation, this group of seven buildings is built upon a small hill. A central wall divides the group into lower and upper sectors, each with an internal plaza. The alignment is north-south with entranceways at buildings 1–5 opening onto the two plazas. Building 6 is round with an inside diameter of 16 feet and its entrance faces south. The north wall has three niches. A single window faces east offering a sightline to Cerro Machu Picchu. The extent of scattered foundations and crumbling, poorly made walls suggest that the lower ridge was a settlement of low-status workers. We later located two additional groups of rectangular houses totaling 33 structures, with more not surveyed in the dense vegetation. The gently sloping and level areas of the long ridge are well suited for agriculture, as demonstrated by several recent cornfields located near the saddle.

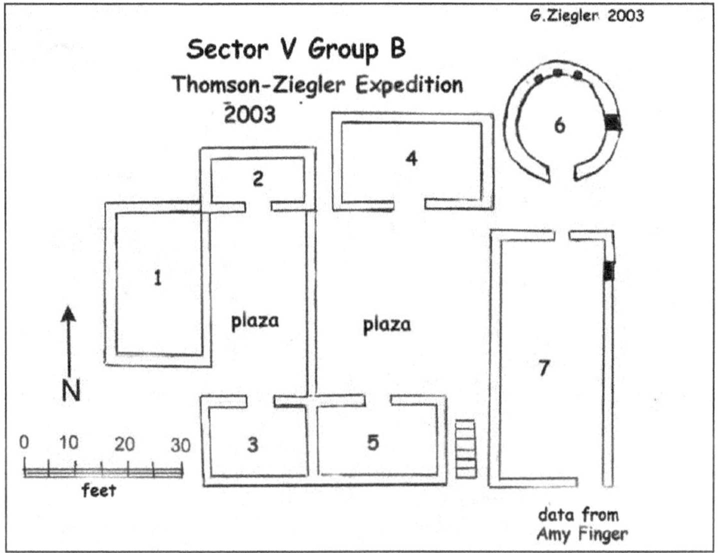

Llactapata Sector V-B site plan. G. Ziegler diagram.

Although Sector V needs considerably more study, two possibilities are that Groups A and B were either storehouse groups *(colcas)* or administrative centers and residences for the local administrators *(caracas).* These were hereditary heads of kinship groups *(ayllus)* that worked and managed agricultural lands. The duality of Andean social organization required two for each settlement (Moseley 1993). If so, Group B could have housed the principal, or more powerful, administrator. The round house with window view of Cerro Machu Picchu may have served a ceremonial function. Tom Zuidema suggests that it may have been a *suntarhuasi*, a round ceremonial structure that most important sites had (Ziegler, personal communication).

Usnu platforms and low walls on the rocky crags above may have offered a view to the east of Cerro Machu Picchu, Veronica, and to the west, Pumasillo. The summit of the big ice peak, Salcantay, can be seen to the south. Reinhard and others have shown these mountains to be particularly important to the Inca. Of interest is that the crags lie exactly on the equinox

Llactapata *usnu* platforms. G. Ziegler photo.

line from near the summit of Veronica. The line crosses the Machu Picchu *Intihuatana* and the summit of Cerro Miguel, which has a platform and upright marker stone on the equinox line (Reinhard 2002). The Sector V platforms may have been especially suited to respect sacred geographical features in combination with equinox alignment and other astronomical phenomena.

Overlook Temple

On the lower ridge above Groups A and B there is an unusual, solitary, two-story structure perched on the edge of a steep drop above the river some 4,000 feet below. Construction is of the finest Vilcabamba style, with larger blocks of shaped quartzite utilized for corners and doorjambs.

The building contains fourteen niches. The one entranceway and two windows open to a balcony or walled, filled platform providing an impressive view of Machu Picchu, the Veronica Range, Cerro San Miguel, Salcantay, and the Urubamba River. The west-facing wall has two open chambers with niches that

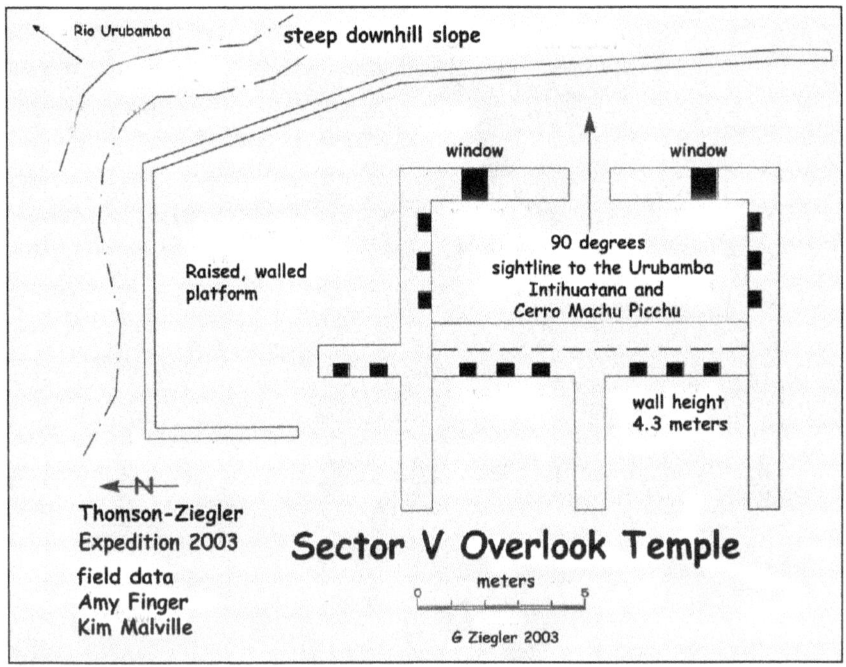

Llactapata Overlook Temple plan. G. Ziegler diagram.

look out on a broad, gently sloping area with no visible evidence of construction. A short wall with two niches extends out 8 feet from the northwest corner, creating an angled passageway leading onto the front platform.

Nearby, a walled path descends toward the Urubamba and the riverside *intihuatana huaca.* The building is cardinal aligned. Its eastern façade and doorway focus a sightline to Machu Picchu Mountain in alignment with the *intihuatana* in the Urubamba Canyon below. This is the line the sun would be seen to follow during equinox for a viewer at any of the three locations. The ice summits of Veronica and Salcantay are also visible. The summit of Cerro San Miguel lies at an azimuth of 60 degrees from the temple. The sun would rise over Huayna Picchu during the June solstice and be seen close to the summit of Cerro San Miguel when first viewed. Both June solstice and equinox ceremonies could be conducted from the temple.

Cerro Machu Picchu viewed from the Overlook Temple at Llactapata.

Tom Zuidema at the Overlook Temple

G. Ziegler photo.

An unusual coincidence of the location of Overlook Temple is that it lies close to the extension of the long axes of the Llactapata Sun Temple (Sector I), the possible *moya* of Sector II, and the *usnu* of Sector III. A person standing on the courtyard of the Sun Temple facing the June solstice sunrise would find the Overlook Temple to be 90 degrees away from the sun. Conversely, a viewer at the Overlook Temple would have the Sun Temple at a right angle to the rising sun during the equinox.

The location at almost the mid-way point between the Overlook Temple and Machu Picchu Mountain would allow an observer to view sunrise near the mountain, and then sunset near the temple during equinox. Reinhard and others have demonstrated the importance of Cerro Machu Picchu to the builders of Machu Picchu (Reinhard 2002; Ziegler and Malville 2006). The placement of the Overlook Temple in relationship to these important features gives it special significance.

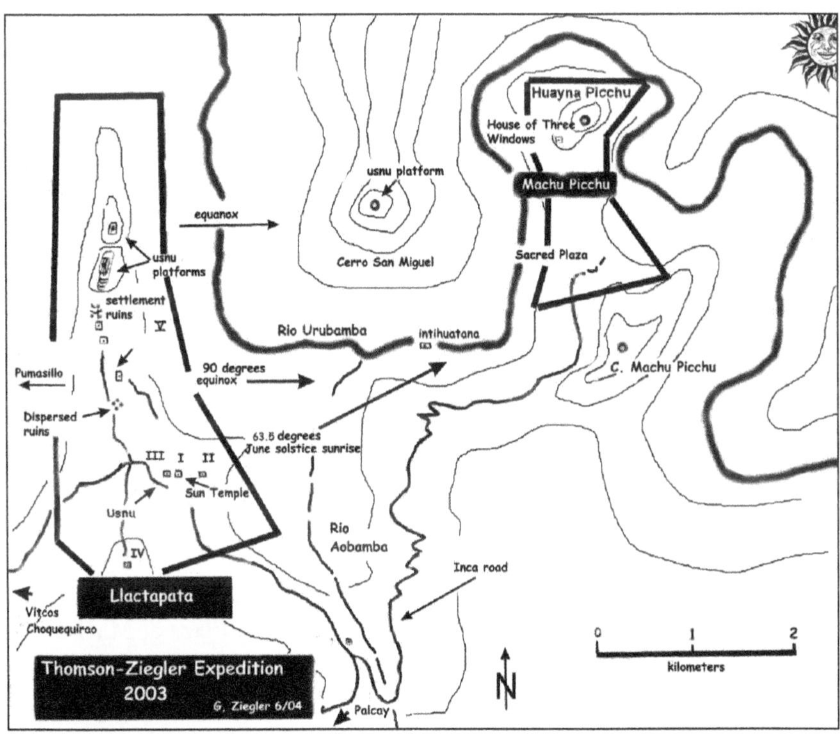

Area archaeological map, Machu Picchu/Llactapata.
G. Ziegler diagram.

Llactapata: Summary and Conclusions

The Thomson-Ziegler Expedition and the later, ongoing Andean Research Project continued by Ziegler with help from Tom Zuidema, Nick Asheshov, David Espejo, John Leivers, Paolo Greer, Edwin Duenas, and many others revealed Llactapata to be a far more substantial site than had previously been realized. As group after group appeared, some uncovered after five centuries of concealment, it became apparent that this was far more than a small compound of buildings described by Hiram Bingham in less than a paragraph.

There are parallels to one of Bingham's most important discoveries, Espíritu Pampa in the Vilcabamba, which he only partially uncovered in 1911. Only later, in 1964, were further sectors revealed and its true significance established—as Vilcabamba (the city), the last refuge of the Inca. Likewise Llactapata, the supposedly insignificant ruin with the unassuming name of "high town" is of much more importance than had been thought. Many groups and features at Machu Picchu have been identified as having alignment to astronomical phenomena or specific topographic features (Dearborn 1981, Reinhard 2002). Johan Reinhard (2002) has suggested that Machu Picchu was located, designed, and functioned as a "sacred center," with a unique convergence of geographical features, sacred mountains, and the Urubamba River, giving astronomical and cardinal alignments. As a closely related satellite of Machu Picchu, this interpretation applies well to the Llactapata complex.

Solstice-equinox orientation in relationship with alignments on Huayna Picchu and Cerro Machu Picchu indicates that adoration and ritual focus on these special mountains and the sun may have been the primary purpose at Llactapata. If the Sector I group is a sun temple as we suggest, its location, situated to view the sun rising over the Sacred Plaza at Machu Picchu midway between the two peaks during the June solstice, gives great ritual importance to the site.

The solitary Overlook Temple seems to be both a June solstice and an equinox feature, placed to view the sun rising near the summits of Cerro San Miguel and Cerro Machu Picchu. The ridge top *usnu* platforms also appear to have an equinox purpose from their placement directly to the west of Cerro San Miguel and Machu Picchu.

The *Usnu* Group in Sector III may also have had an equinox purpose, as the main structures are cardinal aligned. However, the large, raised *usnu* is the principal ceremonial feature. The alignment suggests that the main function may have been December solstice activities. The platform would also have been used for different astronomical and ceremonial events. An alignment relationship with the Overlook Temple and sightlines to and from the Sun Temple, *Usnu* Group, and Sector II is a phenomenon that we suggest was by design.

At Machu Picchu every feature or construction appears to be planned and aligned with a purpose. We suggest that the ceremonial groups and features at Llactapata were placed and built in careful consideration of geo-spiritual and astronomical relationships in conjunction with Machu Picchu. Llactapata was part of a carefully designed network of interrelated administrative and ceremonial sites supporting the regional administrative and ceremonial center at Machu Picchu.

This should be seen in the light of work by John Rowe, Richard Burger, and Lucy Salazar-Burger, which places Machu Picchu in the context of Pachacuti's personal estate (Burger and Salazar-Burger 1993; Rowe 1990). The high-status architecture found not only at Machu Picchu, but throughout the Vilcabamba and at sites along the upper Urubamba Valley, is a reminder of the use of this area for royal estates by the Inca nobility (Burger and Salazar-Burger 1993; Niles 1999).

Llactapata is an important waypoint on a network of roads extending from Cusco to Vitcos and Choquequirao. Our investigations have identified the remnants of an Inca road at Llactapata connecting with the hanging bridge route west from Machu Picchu. Earlier explorations by Hyslop, Lee, Thomson, Ziegler, and others have traced roads from the important Vilcabamba sites of Vitcos and Choquequirao (Hyslop

Inca road view from Llactapata. G. Ziegler photo.

1984; Lee 2000; Thomson 2001; Ziegler 2001). A major road network connecting with extensive Inca-controlled regions to the west reinforces the idea that Machu Picchu was the spiritual and administrative hub of a network of roads, regional settlements, and state-controlled commerce as suggested by Ann Kendall (1988) and others.

A large staging area and meeting hall outside the main gate and a number of *colcas* indicate that Machu Picchu may have been a collecting point for goods arriving from the Vilcabamba to be sent on to the capital or other destinations. If so, Llactapata would have been an important resting place and roadside shrine for important official parties on the road to Machu Picchu and beyond.

Kim Malville at the Machu Picchu drawbridge, where the trail to Llactapata starts. Carlos Aranibar photo.

We have discussed the similarities of Sector II with Wiñay Wayna, which has been identified as a water shrine and resting place on the eastern road (the so-called "Inca trail"). The Sector II group likely served a similar purpose as a sort of high-status *tambo* with seasonal ceremonial activities. The architectural similarities between Sectors I and II reflect the possible division of the site into *hanan* and *hurin* sectors common to pan-Andean societies (Gasparini and Margolies 1980; Hyslop 1990).

An area of about 250 acres suitable for agriculture and the abundance of poorly made structures on the lower ridge in Sector V indicate that quantities of corn and other crops were grown here. American hydrologist Kenneth Wright calculates that the agricultural areas at Machu Picchu could only have produced enough to feed fifty-five people. He estimates that the site housed three hundred permanent residents (Wright and Valencia 2001).

The Llactapata crops may have been a useful way to supplement food production at Machu Picchu. The number of simple foundations suggests that the area was also a low-status settlement that may have housed a population of workers in support of activities at Machu Picchu, just as the settlements in the Cusichaca Valley are thought to have been (Kendall 1988).

We have estimated the distance along the Inca road to Machu Picchu to be around four miles.

The identification and study of the Llactapata archaeological complex adds significantly to our knowledge and understanding of Machu Picchu as the hub of a complex neighborhood of carefully placed, interrelated ceremonial sites reaching outward toward distant imperial Cusco and the far Vilcabamba. The architecture and dramatic landscape of Machu Picchu have always suggested that for the Inca it was a place with considerable depth of meaning and sacred power. Llactapata adds to its significance providing a sun temple, similar to the Coricancha, from which the Pleiades and the June solstice sun rise over Machu Picchu.

Spectacular view of the head of the canyon behind Machu Picchu that separates Machu Picchu from Llactapata. G. Zeigler photo.

Eight
Geology and Design: Shaped Stones, Plaster, and Planning

Machu Picchu view. Hugh Thomson photo.

Machu Picchu

Machu Picchu is built upon a large, wedge-shaped fault block called a graben that was formed by a gradual downward subsidence of the block created by two parallel faults, one near Huayna Picchu and the other near Cerro Machu Picchu. This sinking and erosional process over the past several million years has shaped the stable saddle ridge between the two peaks. The nearby Urubamba River contributed by carving a deep, entrenched meander around the site as continuing tectonic forces slowly lift the mountain mass of the Andes. Numerous lesser faults and subsurface fractures resulting from mountain building pressures are also present.

As base rock is exposed by erosion, these fractures offer zones of weakness subject to ground water penetration and other surface forces that create fragmentation and disintegration into blocks and pieces and eventually, into mixed mineral-organic residue soil. These loose boulders and rocks were the material that supplied building stone for the city.

The regional mountain base is part of an uplifted Paleozoic era, intrusive igneous batholith. These are massive upward traveling bodies of molten material, or magma, that penetrate the upper layers of the earth's surface before stopping short of the surface. Upon cooling they typically leave a shield, or stock-shaped mass, of igneous rock more than 15 square miles in area.

The resulting rock at Machu Picchu is a fine-grained, white-gray granite formed by granules of biotite mica, quartz, and light-colored orthoclase feldspar eroding from an exposed 250 million-year-old batholith pluton. This rock varies in consistency and crystal size. The finest material was selected as building stone for the most important buildings and walls. It is interesting that the massive pluton gives a geological stability to the region, excluding it from tremors and earthquakes that have devastated Cusco on several occasions.

The Inca designers were excellent structural engineers. Analysis of the plaza and the eastern urban sector shows that there has been no movement there in the last five hundred years (Wright and Valencia 2001). As with other Inca sites, special items were made from imported material. Interior pegs at the *wayrona* near the Torreon are made from igneous diorite. Other pegs and stone rings around the city are formed from imported volcanic basalt. Several blocks of reddish rhyolite may have come from Ollantaytambo. Bingham reported finding imported obsidian pebbles and small disks of green chloritic schist of unknown purpose in excavations (Bingham 2002).

The Principle Temple at Machu Picchu. G. Ziegler photo.

Wright and Valencia (2001) write that the House of Three Windows and the Principal Temple at the Sacred Plaza were not completed: "The Principal Temple was not finished because the foundation settled, causing the heavy wall to subside during construction. The builders then abandoned construction. A large stone intended for the temple was left in transit nearby." British geologist Iain Stewart and Gary Ziegler identified several localized fault zones with some indicated slippage eastward from the Sacred Plaza and *Intihuatana* hill while filming a BBC documentary on the Inca and geology there. Several structures show some degree of slippage since their construction.

Temple construction at Ollantaytambo. G. Ziegler photo.

Comparison at the Principle Temple, Machu Picchu. G. Ziegler diagram.

Stewart and Ziegler suggest that subsidence at the Principal Temple occurred after the Inca had abandoned Machu Picchu. As previously mentioned, the Inca builders at the site were superb engineers. This was a most important ceremonial structure that would have had highest priority. If the wall had settled during construction, the builders would have reinforced the foundation and reconstructed the wall.

It seems unlikely that two important temples would have been left uncompleted during the decades of activity and ongoing construction indicated by the archaeological record. At other Inca sites, structures were later modified or removed and replaced by new building. Cusco was rebuilt by the Inca Pachacuti. The principal temple at Ollantaytambo was dismantled and in the process of being rebuilt when abandoned. Construction at Choquequirao shows evidence of later modification (Cieza 1967; COPESCO 1987; Garcilaso 1987).

Choquequirao and Llactapata

The geology of Choquequirao and Llactapata differs significantly from that of Machu Picchu. A deep fault forms the contact between the intrusive pluton and much older central Andean geological structure separating Llactapata and distant Choquequirao from the igneous granite zone. Although only a few miles distant, the Llactapata ridge is composed of metamorphosed, compressed sediments: quartzite, schist, and altered shale with some later igneous activity manifested in isolated intrusive dikes. The present topography has been eroded by the Urubamba River and by rain and breakdown from the nearby peaks, as continuing tectonic forces slowly lift the mountain mass of the Andes.

Glacial processes played a part as well. Numerous faults and subsurface fractures resulting from mountain-building pressures are present (Malville, Thomson, and Ziegler 2004). This description also applies to the Choquequirao ridge, situated in the same formation but shaped by erosional forces associated with the Apurimac drainage and ice peaks nearby.

Construction feature at Ollantaytambo. G. Ziegler photo.

Gary Ziegler (l) and Hugh Thomson (r) at Llactapata, 2003. Amy Finger photo.

Cloud view of the *Intihuatana* at Machu Picchu.
G. Ziegler photo.

Crystalline granite at Machu Picchu was readily worked into multi-angled shapes, blocks, and rounded corners by the hammer-stone pecking method, allowing classic Inca polygonal walls and shaped boulders in abundance. A notable difference between the two royal estates is that Choquequirao has few shaped replica stones, which are in abundance at Machu Picchu.

These were geologically difficult at Choquequirao and Llactapata. The parallel-aligned molecular structure of schist, formed from layers of compressed older sedimentary material, breaks into fragile, flat pieces and slabs. The builders, unable to produce customary imperial monumental architecture, covered the crude-appearing coursed-masonry with rose-colored clay plaster inside and out. Important entranceways and windows requiring rounded edges and large blocks were made from more shapable but less abundant quartzite. Low-status houses at Machu Picchu, made of simple fieldstone *pirca* construction, were also plastered over.

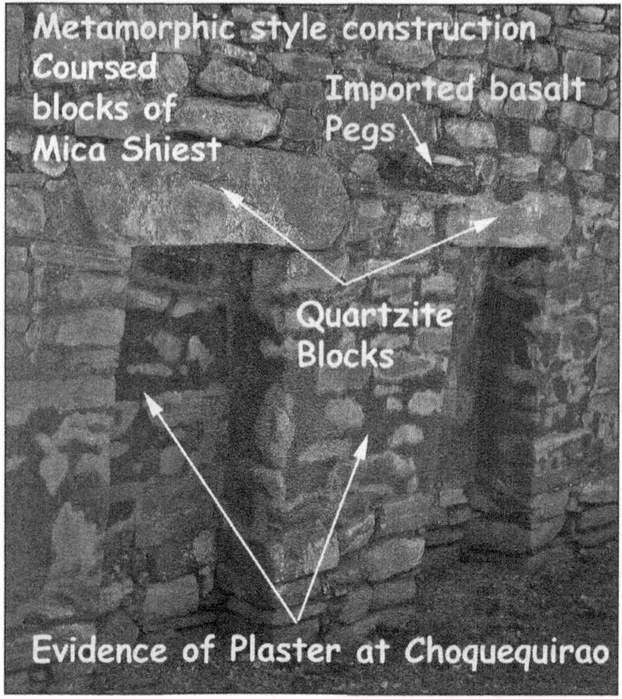

G. Ziegler diagram.

Nine
Summary and Conclusions

We have written in detail about Machu Picchu's spiritually empowered *huacas,* Andean astronomy, *camay,* and the sacred landscape. The descriptions and conclusions relating to Llactapata are summarized in Chapter Seven. This chapter is reserved for the principal focus, the description of and understanding of mystical Choquequirao, Machu Picchu's sacred sister, a royal estate modeled after Machu Picchu, reflecting imperial Inca design and like Machu Picchu, a cloud forest city lost to history.

Choquequirao, the Other Lost City

Experience from our field investigations over the last decade at Llactapata and Machu Picchu leads to the conclusion that important Inca monumental sites were carefully planned and designed in accordance with astronomical alignments, precisely placed in relationship to sacred rivers, mountains, and celestial phenomena (Reinhard 2002; Ziegler and Malville 2006). Choquequirao seems to fit this view. It was uniquely located at a convergence of sacred terrain features with celestial events most important to the Inca state religion and Andean tradition.

The Inca Pachacuti established a pattern for royal estates during the height of imperial Inca expansion across western South America. He constructed estates at Pisac near Cusco, at Ollantaytambo, a preexisting town with ceremonial aspects, and Machu Picchu (Niles 1999; Rostworowski 1983; Rowe 1990). The impressive estates at Pisac and Machu Picchu seem to have established a pattern followed at Choquequirao.

Important, high-status construction is centered on a ridge top with a higher mountain behind and a lower distinctive promontory in front, with a sacred river flowing below in view. Each hosts a series of fountains or baths passing through the ridge top groups.

Pachacuti's successor, Topa Inca Yupanki, expanded the imperial reach well beyond the borders of present day Peru. With a desire to establish his own estates, he secured holdings not far from Cusco, the most notable being highland Chinchero (Niles 1999). Viewing Pachacuti's magnificent mountain estate, Machu Picchu, he may have felt pressure to create something of equal grandeur. The resistant Chachapoya in northern Peru were first contacted at this time and later incorporated into the expanding Inca Empire by the Inca Huayna Capac (D'Altroy 2003; RGI 1557[21]).

Moving colonists around the realm was an established Inca policy, particularly those with skills needed for a particular project. As architectural style of several important features at Choquequirao appears to be of Chachapoya design, it is probable that early imported Chachapoya workers were responsible. There is good evidence that Chachapoya groups were settled in the region. This suggests that Inca state administration under Topa Inca initiated the construction of Choquequirao.

Huayna Capac established an estate near Urubamba but concentrated on conquering far Ecuador, where he was building a second capital city. It seems unlikely that he would have undertaken another major project in isolated Vilcabamba. The timing, plus the aforementioned architectural features, indicate Topa Inca as the builder of Choquequirao. We suggest that Topa Inca had Choquequirao built as his own Machu Picchu. Although Choquequirao is ideally located on a narrow ridge above the Apurimac and surrounded by snow peaks, Topa Inca and his builders must have been disappointed with the fragile metamorphic rock at the site.

Machu Picchu incorporates in-situ igneous granite boulders

that are shaped to replicate surrounding mountains throughout the site. These ceremonially important features were difficult to include when building Choquequirao. As a royal estate during the height of the empire, Choquequirao would have likely served as a provincial administrative center, as did some other estates (Niles 1999).

Evidence that coca was widely grown, the coca storehouses at Hurincancha, the llama pens at Cotacoca, and the llama train mural support Choquequirao as an important coca growing and distribution center (Paz 2004). Intensive cultivation with ongoing construction and maintenance would have required a large resident population. The large mountainside settlement above the temple water shrine of Pinchaunuyoc would have housed the needed workers well away from privileged resident Inca administrators, attendants, and main group temples.

Notes

21. A sixteenth-century document from Chachapoyas recorded in Relaciones Geographicas de Indias (RGI 1557) states that Topa Inca visited the region claiming lands near Moyobamba. This helps to establish that Topa Inca had the opportunity to import Chachapoya workers to the Inca heartland and Choquequirao before Huayna Capac later subdued the resistant Chachapoya polity.

Ten
Trekking Routes, Field Notes, and Exploring Guide to Choquequirao

One of the rewards of visiting Choquequirao is that it has remained well off of the beaten path. Only a few hundred people visit during the dry season as compared to two thousand daily at Machu Picchu. Arriving by the shortest route requires two days of strenuous hiking. Descending into the deep Apurimac then back up some 4,500 feet to reach the site is like crossing Arizona's Grand Canyon. One either carries a heavy backpack or hires local packers to bring the needed supplies with horses or mules.

The best solution is to sign on with one of the Cusco-based trekking agencies that regularly take small groups of two to six there during the dry season months of April into December. It is possible to ride a horse most of the way on all but the shortest route, which goes directly up from the Apurimac River below Huanipaca, but good horses are hard to come by. Most of the local packers' stock is not up to standards of safety and dependability, nor are they well cared for. Some trekking agencies are marginal. A good test is the cost. If it seems really cheap, there is a reason. We recommend careful research and references before signing on.

Trails starting from four places eventually lead to Choquequirao, which now can be viewed on Google Maps. Each offers a uniquely different route and experience. A brief gen-

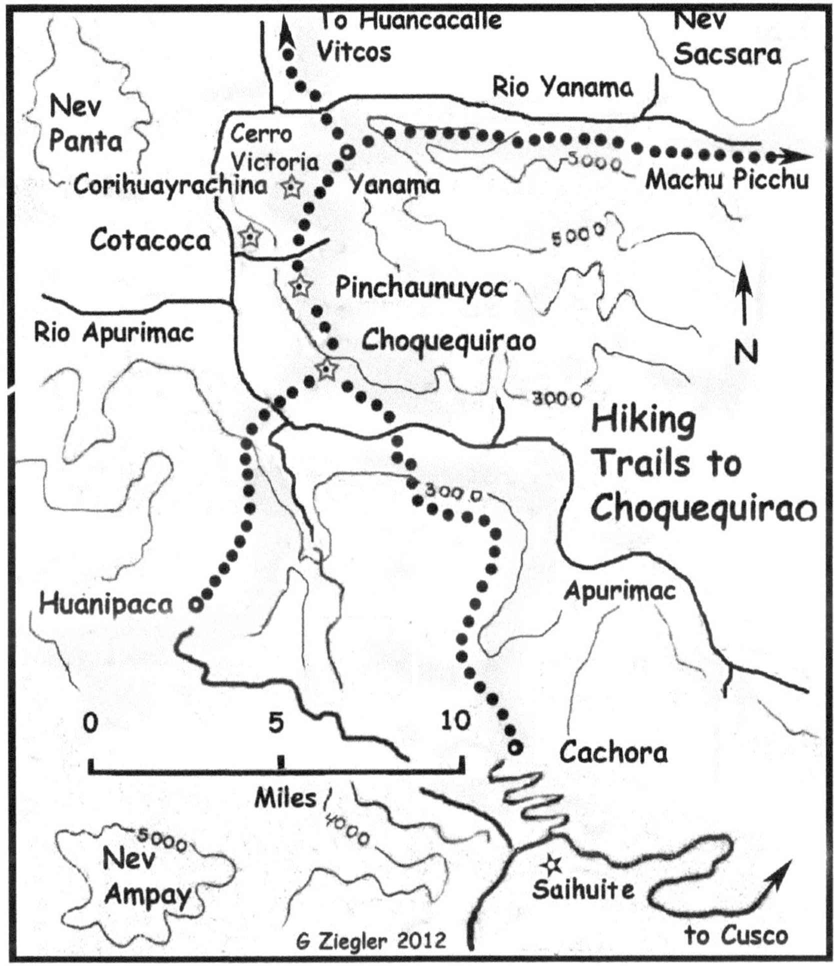

Map illustration of routes to Choquequirao. G. Ziegler diagram.

eral description and comments from our many years of travel along these routes follow. This is not a complete guide but may help with planning and preparation.

Route One: Cachora to Choquequirao

The small community of Cachora sits in a lush, broad valley leading down to an immensely steep drop to the Apurimac River. Agriculture and travel in the valley goes back to pre-Inca

Guided Treks, Horse Trips, Expedition Planning, and Filming Support

Adventure Specialists' ranch *chacra* and horses above Cusco

E Duenas photo

Edwin and Fanny Duenas manage Adventure Specialists Peru. Amy Finger manages Adventure Specialists USA, based at the historic 1880s Bear Basin Ranch in the Colorado Rocky Mountains. They operate historical and culturally focused trips on horseback in Colorado, Argentina, Mexico's Copper Canyon, Spain's Pyrenees, and Peru. Adventure Specialists may be the founders of adventure travel in Peru, having trained the first guides and formed the first agency in 1970. They now focus on custom itineraries for small groups, archaeology, documentary films, deluxe Andean treks, and Inca research. They offer personal service and ultra-quality programs that only a small, highly experienced, motivated, enthusiastic group can offer.

Adventure Specialists' home in Peru is a ranch near Cusco where they maintain a well-trained *remuda* of quality trail horses. The horses are used for Choquequirao, the Classic Inca Trail inn-to-inn ride, custom treks, and archaeological tours. They also operate vehicle-supported regional visits, light hiking to archaeological sites, and day horse trips to sites near Cusco. They are happy to share advice, current travel information, and help plan itineraries.

Adventure Specialists USA
US phone 719-783-2076
info@adventurespecialists.org
www.adventurespecialists.org

times. The present colonial-period community was established as a part of Hernando Pizarro's holdings, or *encomienda*, in the mid-1500s. Life here was pretty much unchanged until the Maoist terrorist group, Sendero Lumino, took violent control in the 1980s. Many villagers with training or education were rounded up and executed as a prelude to establishing absolute control. We heard these horror stories when visiting there just after government troops and national police evicted the Senderos following the capture of Sendero leader Abimael Guzman in 1992.

Work at Choquequirao and growing tourism has put the community back on track. In 1995, the government Choquequirao project completed a new trail with a suspension bridge crossing the Apurimac River. This permitted loaded pack horses to travel back and forth from Cachora. Traveling from Cusco, allow the better part of a day to arrive at Cachora. As of this writing, it takes five to six hours. The highway access regularly slides away with slow, repair-created detours and hosts increasing heavy truck traffic.

Some of the route has returned to potholes and extreme dust. No solution has appeared to solve these delays. Highways can't be built to hold on steep, unstable, Andean mountain slopes. Of course, the Inca knew this and carefully placed their foot and pack llama-traveled roads up, down, and around where modern roads won't work. The Cachora road turns off of the mostly paved Central Highway several miles past the Inca monument of Saihuite, to wind down several thousand feet to the community. There are a few small, rustic places to stay with basic Andean food: chicken, soups, and beer.

Although serious trekkers can reach the camp at Choquequirao in one horrendous, long day, two days is the reasonable norm. A minimum of six days should be allowed for a visit and round trip from Cachora. The usually well-maintained trail follows along the rim of the Apurimac Canyon with considerable ups and downs before finally dropping steeply to the river and bridge.

View of the Apurimac and the trail to Cachora. Paolo Greer photo.

There are two suitable places to camp. The first is high up before the drop to the river. Someone has built a couple of shelters there with cold showers and piped-in water. There are ample flat places for tents. Usually someone is there to sell beer or Inca Kola. The second camp is at the river. COPESCO built a structure there for housing workers while building the bridge. As of this writing, it has been renovated and is serviceable. There are plenty of tent sites and one can cool off in the river. It is hot at an elevation of around 5,000 feet. The vegetation looks like the Sonoran Desert, with cactus and thorny acacia trees. Small biting gnats lurk in ambush so bring repellant, long sleeves, and a closable tent.

The trail switchbacks steeply up after the bridge, climbing steadily until arriving at Choquequirao. Several small *chacras* are passed along the way, and higher up are small clusters of houses, fields, and corrals. A campsite with water and a latrine has been built about an hour or so from the archaeological complex, where one can camp for a small fee. Just before reaching the edge of the designated zone, the INC, now Ministry of Culture (MC), has placed a small toll booth where a fee is collected. As of our last visit in 2013, it was forty Soles (about $17), which is probably justified by the new camping site with flush toilets and a cold-water shower house.

From the camp, it is easy to follow the pathways around the main groups, which are marked by signs. Carry this book with you to help identify the groups, structures, and alignments of the various buildings, walls, and features. Visiting the distant groups of Capullyoc, Hurincancha, or the Casa Cascada may require a guide. Allow most of a day for any of these. Llamayoc can be seen in an hour or two, as it is close down from the Lower Plaza.

A reality of trail travel in the steep Andes is that slides and floods frequently remove sections of trails. During May of 2011, a tremendous rockslide briefly blocked the Apurimac River, which backed up to destroy the bridge on the Choquequirao route from Cachora.

Field Notes from the April 2013 Andean Research Project

April 25: Traveling to Choquequirao and Cachora, Homeward Bound

The day broke bright and clear—*espejado*—as we say in the equatorial Andes. After a brilliant Andean sunrise, our sunrise photographers returned and camp was packed. All then mounted the now rested, energized horses to trot cheerfully along good, near-level, trail traversing high above the roaring Apurimac River below.

Later today, we must descend to the river and cross on a swaying cable-suspended box. Some seemed to greet this expectation with limited enthusiasm. Today's journey is comparable to a crossing of the Grand Canyon but by now all are fit and comfortable with long descents and slow, steady climbs. We ride when we can, but like me, some walk much of the way, particularly on steep difficult trail. Anyway, it is good to have a trusty, calm mount to hop on when the need moves you. More, we carried no day packs or gear, which is stashed in the ample saddle bags traveling nearby when needed. I traveled light, wearing running shoes with legs protected for riding by leather gaiters called "half chaps" in the riding trade. These serve well for hiking through brush and snake country as well.

Several hours travel downhill placed us at the trail's end—bridge abutments with forlornly sagging cables and alas, no flooring. The bridge was gone. We were scheduled to visit Choquequirao last May when word came down that the bridge was out. Now we see the reason: An immense rockslide had dammed up the Apurimac just downriver, creating a dam that backed up water to the bridge, destroying planking and lower supports.

Choquequirao was effectively closed except for hardy travelers coming and going by the long arduous route in and out via Yanama. There weren't many last year. This reflects a millennium of hard life in the Andes. It has never been easy and the natural environment is cruel to the careless or unfortunate. Civilizations have come and gone here, even for the privileged. We are happy to just cross the river on whatever means available. That means is an *oroya* [a long swinging cable and a small box-like contraption attached on pulleys, with a pull rope] to haul one across above the raging rapids. Our trusted horses and pack stock were necessarily left behind.

New mounts—sturdy mules and saddle horses—awaited us on the far bank if we successfully survived the cable crossing, which I can hap-

Crossing the Apurimac on a cable *oroya*. Ken Greenwood photo.

pily report we did. We faced bonding with a new wrangler crew and unknown new equines. But, this is the stuff of adventure. All rose admirably to the occasion. We were soon sharing tales in a comfortable camp some distance up from the buggy river bottom on an ancient, pre-Inca, breezy plateau, recently developed as a tourist encampment with running water and bottled beer. They even have a flush toilet marginally in operation, although several of us opted for the nearby woods. In either case, the local mosquitoes relished the opportunity for exposed bottoms.

April 26: Enough Time in the Wilds

"The bright lights of Cusco are shining like diamonds, like ten thousand jewels in the sky." We mount up or strike out walking. It is a mere 4,000 feet uphill and 12 miles to our awaiting transport at the village of Cachora. We got it done without mishap. Evening finds us enjoying a late meal in Cusco's favorite pub. It was a great, successful adventure ...

Route Two: Huanipaca to Choquequirao

The road to Huanipaca leaves the Central Highway a few miles after the Cachora turnoff. Travel time is about an hour more than to Cachora. Huanipaca, another small colonial-period town, is situated similarly in a broad, lush valley descending to the Apurimac River. The road is driveable some distance down the valley past the town, winding past fields of maize, quinoa, oats, and grazing cows to finally reach a trailhead at a point where the valley narrows into a steeply descending canyon.

The trail is in good shape and well traveled down to the old hacienda of San Ignacio. From there, a less-traveled trail drops steeply another 1,000 feet down to the Apurimac River through eucalyptus, cactus, and tall agave, reminiscent of the Sierra Madre of Mexico. Some investor group, envisioning Machu Picchu and hordes of tourists, has built a small riverside camp with showers, kitchen, and even flush toilets. Like many such projects in the Andes, it now lies abandoned. The toilets no longer flush, but it serves as a good camp for the night.

Crossing a swaying, primitive, suspension bridge built by the same visionaries, the trail continues—blasted and hacked out of the sheer cliff face, held in place by steel rods drilled

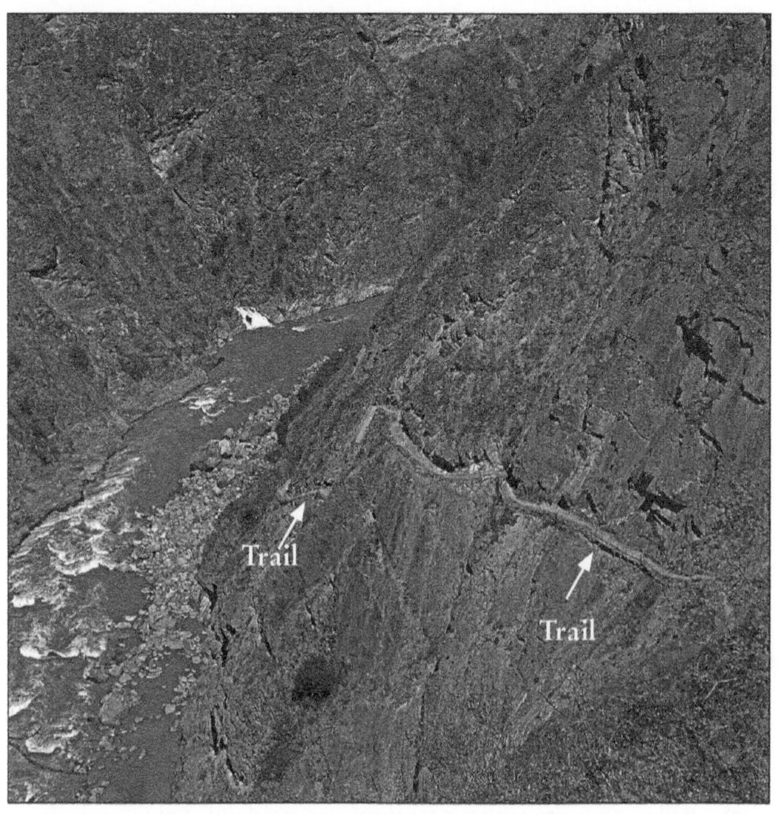

View of the Huanipaca hanging trail. G. Ziegler photo.

into the hard metamorphic rock for some distance above the bridge. Eventually, it reaches a gentler slope, gaining firm footing to zigzag upward. Although reasonably safe for foot traffic, only the most sure-footed and dependable pack stock can be brought on this route. Someone has placed a "No horses" sign along the trail when leaving Choquequirao.

The vegetation changes from microclimate—semi-arid cactus and acacia—to dense Andean cloud forest as the trail gains elevation. Resident flocks of Andean parakeets squawk noisily alone the way. A determined, steady climb of three to four hours gains Choquequirao's Lower Plaza. The camping site is another thirty minutes away. The climb is about 4,500 feet up from the river.

Note: This route washed out in 2012, so it may not always be open. If you plan to travel without a guide service, always ask around Cusco for the status of trails before starting out.

A cable car is being proposed to bring more tourist groups to Choquequirao. As unlikely as it sounds, if constructed, it would probably use this route as being the shortest and most direct. The remoteness and undeveloped aspect of this unique royal estate is one of the main attractions and a rewarding adventure for those who travel the rugged terrain to reach Choqueauirao. Although the distance from Cusco and the travel time required would likely limit the number of visitors, the site would lose much of its charm. An overview of the current Machu Picchu experience in comparison follows.

Field Notes from the April 2013 Andean Research Project

Machu Picchu is overrun because accessibility is made easy by the railroad, offering comfortable one-day travel from Cusco. An ascetic, contemplative visit now seems impossible. Large tour groups block the narrow passages, dominating the paths and features. Many are thirty participants or more, led by guides carrying tall flags so they won't be lost in the mob. Multitudes of Ministry of Culture *chalecoed* [vested] guardians lurk everywhere, blowing seemingly continuous shrill whistle blasts at confused tourists who may have strayed from the arrow-marked path blocked by the large groups. Worse, the *Intihuatana* stone, which many of us consider the most important sacred, *huaca* feature at Machu Picchu, is now roped off to only a narrow walkway on one side. A newly posted sign states "Keep Moving," without even the courtesy of a "please." The once enjoyable side-visit up Huaynu Picchu or distant Cerro Machu Picchu is now prohibited unless one purchases an additional ticket below in Aguas Calientes before arrival. I wonder when they will charge additional to visit the *Intihuatana*? Choquequirao and other lesser-known sites are unlikely to suffer the Disneyland degradation and exploitation of Machu Picchu. The more accessible trek routes will become fewer, but some remote ones will remain. There will always be something for the adventurous traveler to explore, away from the madness of Machu Picchu.

Route Three: Huancacalle-Vitcos to Choquequirao

Day 1. It is a long day by road from Cusco to Huancacalle. The highway from Cusco crosses over Malaga Pass after passing through the narrow, congested center of Ollantaytambo. Crossing the Urubamba River at Chaullay, the location of a former Inca bridge, a secondary road, when not blocked by frequent slides, continues up the Vilcabamba River Valley, finally arriving at the small community of Huancacalle.

The only suitable and preferred place to stay is the Sixpac Manco hostel, home of the Cobos Family. Members of the family have outfitted and accompanied every major expedition in the Vilcabamba, starting with Gene Savoy's 1964 legendary exploration and identification of Espiritu Pampa as Vilcabamba, Bingham's allusive lost city. Juvenal Cobos was with Gary Ziegler on his first expedition in 1965. The family has worked extensively with Vince and Nancy Lee over the years. The Lees generously raised funding for the Sixpac Manco lodge, remaining in contact with the family and close friends.

G. Ziegler filming at Vitcos, 1994. Amy Finger photo.

Day 2. A stay at Huancacalle necessitates a day or more visiting nearby Vitcos and the White Rock, also known as Nusta Hispanan or Yuroc Rumi, made famous by Hugh Thomson's book of the same name and Bingham's earlier description of his visit there. A short, two-hour hike leads to Cerro Rosaspata and the ruins of Vitcos, the palace refuge of Manco and the

The White Rock shrine, Yuroc Rumi near Vitcos
It is also known as Nusta Hispanan
A shaped replication of the mountain
on the horizon
G Ziegler 1965

last Inca. Manco was killed here in 1544 by befriended Spanish refuges from the colonial civil wars. Captured and looted by Garcia de Loyola under orders of Viceroy Toledo in 1572, Vitcos remains seldom visited. The massive, shaped White Rock boulder *huaca* and its temple remains can be seen in the same day.

Day 3. Leaving from the Cobos lodge at the end of the road on the far southern edge of town, the route follows an abandoned mining road up a long, broad valley, then it becomes a well-traveled but poorly maintained trail around cliffs and muddy bogs. The best camp is on a high *pampa* before the trail starts steeply up the pass *(abra)*. A wide Inca road (Inca *nan)* is visible here as an elevated causeway across the boggy *pampa.*

Day 4. Following along the well-preserved, stone-paved Inca road over the 15,200–foot high Choqueticarpo Pass, the trail descends a broad glacier-sculpted valley overhung by towering granite pinnacles. A small group of rounded ruins can be explored below the top of the pass, which probably was a stopover and supply point *tambo.* Curiously, two parallel roads, one on each side of the valley, climb up to merge at the pass. The high point has a small platform *usnu* and piles of stones *(apachitas)* offered by travelers to the mountain spirits *(apu)* of the region.

Camp can be made among large granite boulders below the massive fluted glaciers of Nevado Pumasillo. One of the world's most beautiful mountains, Pumasillo, in Quechua means the "puma's claw." We call this the "refrigerator camp" due to very cold nights and frosted tents in the morning.

Day 5. Crossing another high ridge over to the Yanama Valley, the trail passes by several small farms, or *chacras*—cultural remnants of the distant past. These people live much the same as their ancestors, planting potatoes with a digging stick while keeping a rugged Andean existence tolerable with coca and corn beer *(chicha)*. Camp can be set up at several flat areas around Yanama on dramatic high spots overlooking the village and its picturesque valley. Expect a long day.

Elevated Inca road at Choqueticarpo Pass. G. Ziegler photo.

Day 6. Another major Inca road joins at Yanama. The route climbs 3,000 feet up a precipitous trail carved through the cliffs of San Juan Pass to abandoned silver mines at Mina Victoria. From our explorations at Cotacoca, downstream on the Yanama River, we know that the main Inca road followed the canyon and river to Cotacoca then back up to Pinchaunuyoc and on to Choquequirao. This high road going over San Juan Pass is from the colonial period and was used for working the extensive drift and tunnel mine works. The Inca had secondary trails to the mineral deposits and on to Cerro Victoria.

A first view of the immense Apurimac drainage far below

is seen from the pass. This deep canyon and its powerful river is one of the great geographic wonders of the Americas. The Apurimac thunders hundreds of miles through the remotest part of the Andes to eventually, along with a multitude of sister rivers, become the Amazon. From the pass, the trail winds down 3,000 feet to the only suitable camp at Maizal, a small farm carved out of the precipitous mountainside by the Valentin Saca family in the 1990s. Seeking land to homestead, they returned to settle here following work with us on earlier trail clearing and explorations. The National Geographical Society Corihuayrachina project was based here in 2001.

If time permits, it is worth another day for a visit to the hillsides below Cerro Victoria. This rugged region is dotted with round foundations, looted tombs, and an *usnu* platform high up on the ridges (Victoria's Secret). Much is now overgrown but it offers grand views and a taste of extreme archaeology in the Andes. In true exploring tradition, we have seen the rare spectacled bear, encountered poisonous snakes, and enjoyed condors riding thermals up from the heated canyon below here.

Field Notes Excerpt

Most structures at Corihuayrachina are circular, many with low walls of 2 feet or less. These are common throughout the Vilcabamba. We have always thought that these were pre-Inca, but here we have Inca or Inca-influenced pottery found within the floor debris. One of the groups is clearly rectangular Inca architecture and a well-made rectangular building, which we think is a *colca* [storehouse], sits high up on the slopes of Cerro Victoria.

I believe that most of the round structures that I examined were dwellings, but there were several types and sizes in different locations. Some were simple low-wall affairs that I believe served as retaining platforms for wooden houses now long gone. Other large ones could have been corrals for llamas. Some features, such as the large ridgetop platforms, are ceremonial but we found no obvious ceremonial architecture within the complex. Our consensus for the moment is that the rectangular group represents an Inca administrative center within a settlement of imported foreign workers, or *Mitayos*.

Burial chamber at Corihuayrachina. G. Ziegler photo.

We examined what seems like an unusual number of burial mounds and chambers scattered throughout the site. All were low-status, containing human remains and few burial accoutrements such as pots, tools, or ornaments that are normally expected in such burials. This influenced our opinion that the inhabitants, at least the ones that were interred here, had very few possessions.

The Saca family farm is also the jumping-off point for a primitive trail descending to Cotacoca in the depths of the Yanama Canyon. This requires several more days but offers an exceptional adventure to a truly lost world where few have ventured during the last four hundred years.

Field Notes

The Cotacoca site lies at 1850m (GPS map location: 18L 0727848-UTM 8521494) near the junction of the Yanama and Blanco Rivers. It is on an isolated bench or mesa about a mile long, left as an eroded remnant when the Rio Yanama river cut a deep chasm near its intersection with the Rio Blanco. This area of the Vilcabamba is characterized by the deep canyons that rivers, such as the Apurimac and Urubamba, have made through the mountain ranges on their rapid descent to the

Amazon Basin. The valley bottom at Cotacoca is hot and semi-tropical with a microclimate environment created by the deep canyon. Like the nearby Inca site of Choquequirao, the bedrock is an assortment of metamorphic muscovite schist and fine-grained yellow quartzite. A considerable depth of alluvial deposit swept in by river flooding and canyon breakdown covers the valley floor. Much of this material is made up of igneous grey granite in the form of rounded river stones that have been carried downstream.

An initial clearance showed that Cotacoca contains at least thirty stone-built structures, including a 75-foot long *kallanca* [meeting hall] grouped around a great central plaza, with some walls standing to a height of almost 10 feet.

Day 7. Leaving the farm, the main trail descends, seemingly forever, to a rocky, flood-eroded canyon several thousand feet below. After crossing the small Rio Blanco, a narrow pathway cuts through near-vertical colluvium cliffs to less dangerous slopes above. Several pack animals have fallen here. It is not a route for the timid. Pinchaunuyoc, the unusual terraces and water temple described in Chapter Two, lies some 2,000 feet above. There is room here to place tents near the only water source for a comfortable camp and needed rest. The site can be explored after arrival or before departing the next morning.

Field Notes from the April 2013 Andean Research Project

April 22: Completing a hot, buggy descent to the river in the morning, the Rio Blanco was crossed and the steep climb, more than 2,000 feet to the next camp at Pinchaunuyoc, was completed by mid-afternoon. We hiked most of the trail, as it's too steep and narrow to be safely negotiated while mounted, earning an early Happy Hour in an outrageously spectacular setting. The next morning, following ample coffee and breakfast, we thoroughly examined the multiple terraces, water features, and several shrine structures that make up Pinchaunuyoc, an unusual, monumental site seemingly in the middle of nowhere. In actuality, it was the spiritually symbolic main entrance portal to Choquequirao.

We carefully examined the recently reconstructed walls, which I am comparing with my original photos and diagrams from first clearing the

Hugh Thomson and team at Cotacoca. G. Ziegler photo.

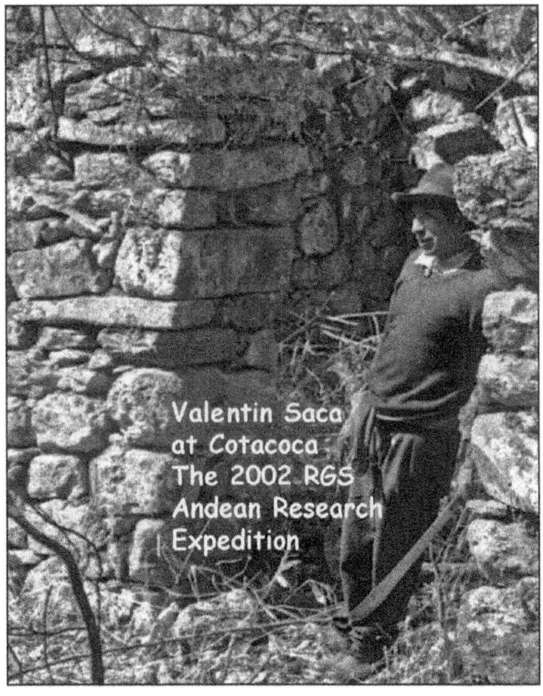

G. Ziegler photo.

Trail below Pinchaunuyoc with horses. Lillian Roberts photo.

G. Ziegler at the main temple at Pinchaunuyoc. Lillian Roberts photo.

site many years ago. Inca authority Vince Lee and our team both previously mapped and diagramed the site, giving excellent documentation. We made additional measurements, verified angles and azimuths, and collected more photos before moving on. Arriving mid-afternoon at Choquequirao, the team settled in for cold showers at the new government campsite, a rest, and then lively discussion of the journey's events over Happy Hour. Our cooks, Poncho and Andy, whipped up tasty appetizers accompanying before-dinner wine and stronger distillates.

Day 8. Today is the final 3,000-foot climb to an unnamed pass, then a gradual drop through dense cloud forest to arrive at Choquequirao by mostly following the original and only Inca road to the royal estate. There is much to see along the way—round house settlements, stone terraces, and a nicely constructed and placed group we simply named Patawasi, or "high house."

Route Four: Machu Picchu to Choquequirao

Day 1. Starting from the town of Aguas Calientes, the staging point for visitors to Machu Picchu, there are two options: A daily local train goes to the hydroelectric plant at the end of the line or one can walk the six miles down the tracks at anytime. The cost for the short 20-minute train trip is $20 as of this writing. The walk down is worth the view of the sheer backside of Machu Picchu and a cacophony of cloud forest bird calls along the riverbank. From Hydroelectrica, a new road follows the Urubamba River a short distance to the larger town of Santa Teresa. There are small places to stay and assorted chicken and soup eateries.

Option two is to hike over the Llactapata ridge in one long day and camp at the community of Lucmabamba some distance up the Santa Teresa Valley. The Llactapata archaeological complex has recently been included in the park system, which now limits camping. Sadly, it also prohibits a visit or study of the site. The 3,000-foot up and back down with more than ten miles of hiking leaves little time to see the various groups. The buildings and walls, with the exception of a part of the

Panoramic view from Patawasi above Pinchaunuyoc. Hugh Thomson photo.

Sun Temple group, have not been cleared, reinforced, restored, or otherwise protected. Cattle wander freely through the area. As of this writing, a few trekking visitors are allowed to camp overnight with the cows at the one suitable campsite with water. We are fortunate to have completed the studies, diagrams, site maps, photos, and accumulated data of this important Inca ceremonial complex and extenuation of Machu Picchu before it was lost again in the dense cloud forest.[22]

Day 2. A truck ride can be arranged from Santa Teresa or Lucmabamba up the valley. The road continues to the next recommended camp at Tortora. Although it is possible to hire a truck, the road is occasionally blocked and impassable when it rains much. One can also hike to Tortora in a long day from Lucmabamba. Santa Teresa can also be reached by a road that follows the Urubamba River up-canyon from the town of Chaullay, branching off from the road to Huancalle and Vitcos, in a long day from Cusco or Ollantaytambo.

Day 3. The hike from Tortora continues along a major Inca route coming from the east and the ice peak Salkantay. The well-traveled trail crosses over a 16,400-foot pass, then drops down a long, moist, alpine valley between the spectacular ice peaks of Nevado Quisahua to the south and the Sacsara Summits to the north. The next camp is at the village of Yanama. The Inca road south from Huancacalle joins here. As of this writing, the road has been completed over the pass to Yanama.

Field Notes from the April 2013 Andean Research Project

After enjoying evening dinner and drinks at the bustling, tourist-laden Aguas Calientes, we elected to walk downriver six miles the following morning, satisfyingly avoiding the absurdly overpriced train to the new road connection at Hydroelectrica. Our camp gear and transport van met us there. We drove several hours up the Santa Teresa Valley to the small Andean community of Tortora. The new road is rough and barely passible. Camp was set in a flat field alongside grazing pack mules, saddle horses, and the trusted wrangler crew we had arranged to meet there.

April 20: After packing and breakfast, we set out on horseback with pack train in tow along the old Inca trail winding up and over 16,400-foot high Yanama Pass. The trail was sadly destroyed in many places, along with ancient pre-Inca walls and structures, by freshly bulldozed rockslides along the new road. The road had already been blocked or slid away in a number of places during the recent rainy season. These previous cuts were now abandoned and a new route freshly carved out, sometimes on the opposite side of the ascending valley, accompanied by immense rock and gravel slides streaming hundreds of feet downslope.

We were aghast at the damage. Who is paying for this, we wondered? Who authorized it? Where is the Ministry of Culture, tasked by national law to prevent archaeological destruction? Continuing over the pass, the destruction is worse. The road cuts through a centuries-old Inca *usnu* platform and ancient *apachitas* [rock-offering mounds] that had adorned the crest. Looking down the valley of the Yanama River, the view is dominated by long switchbacks—some more than half a mile—and huge road-debris waste slides. We know from research that this valley was the Inca route to Choquequirao. The upper valley below the pass contains vast pastures, remains of corrals, and extensive crumbled walls built to contain large llama herds that transported the empire's valued coca produce from the fields and storage houses of the royal estate and regional ceremonial center, Choquequirao.

Later we came to the end of the road approaching the community of Yanama, but still lacking a half-mile or so to go. A lone, big D-8 bulldozer was surging away along the hillside attended by a supply and fuel vehicle, curiously with Mountain Lodge's logo emblazoned on its side. Are they supporting and funding this?

Day 4–7. Yanama to Choquequirao: See the Route Three description for days 6–8.

Road damage at Yanama Pass. Steve Bein photo.

Yanama Pass

new road

Inca road

pre -Inca ruins

Road damage at Yanama Pass. Steve Bein photo.

Bulldozing in the Yanama Valley. Paolo Greer photo.

Notes

22. Our explorations and investigations at Llactapata were authorized by the regional Cusco office of the Instituto Nacional de Cultura (INC) by then Director, David Ugarte. The permit excluded excavation and collection of material, which was not relevant to the surface survey and documentation.

Acknowledgments

A network of support, encouragement, and teamwork
Gary Ziegler

This is a difficult chapter to write. So many have generously contributed so much—knowledge, encouragement, observations, data, funding, support, team work, efforts, and skills beyond description. The list is lengthy. We are certainly destined to leave some of the deserving unrecognized. Please accept our apology as we highlight but a few that we have worked most closely with.

G. Ziegler at Espiritu Pampa, 1965. Jorge Moreau photo.

My archaeological adventures and studies in Peru began some decades ago when I organized my first expedition to Espiritu Pampa as a very young grad student at Peru's San Marcos University. Since those days, I have pursued several different lives but always returning periodically to the Andes in search of mysteries to solve, and yes, savor the adventure. It has always been a team effort reflecting the philosophical belief that a whole is greater than the sum of its parts. The information and conclusions of this writing are a composite gathered from those who have worked, studied, investigated, suffered the bugs, danger, cold rains, and altitude on our expeditions and on their own.

A remarkable phenomenon of this sort of extreme archaeology is that all have generously and freely shared their work with the rest, not a common occurrence in the broader scientific community. **Kim Malville** and I worked as Outward Bound instructors in the formative days of that organization at home in Colorado coercing reluctant, privileged youth and ghetto survivors together up high peaks. Meanwhile, Kim progressed to a deserved position as Chair of the University of Colorado's Astro-Geophysics department.

Kim Malville Working at Llactapata Camp June 2003

Years later, we reconnected to form a multidiscipline team put together for the Llactapata project near Machu Picchu. As an accomplished leader in the evolving field of archaeoastronomy, Kim elevated me from archaic terrestrial limitations to look also toward the heavens. Much of what we have learned about Inca site placement, design, and ceremonial architectural alignment comes from Kim's astute observations and celestial measurements. We owe the most to dedicated expedition and research partners. We have struggled together against some of the worst that the high Andean terrain and weather could throw at us and hopefully, have made a significant contribution to the understanding of the ancient cultures of the Andes. We have all become friends in the process.

Hugh Thomson has been the mover and shaker of the projects. He is an inexhaustible, careful researcher, acclaimed author, award-winning filmmaker, and intrepid explorer of the old school. Hugh started out as a student apprentice with Ann Kendall on her Cusichaca project years back. Hugh and I connected as kindred spirits somewhere around Vitcos in the mid-1990s. I showed him Puncuyoc and the mysteries of the Inca routes to Choquequirao from the north. We later teamed up for the Cotacoca expedition and work at Choquequirao and Llactapata. Hugh introduced me to John Hemming and the Royal Geographical Society, invaluable resources that have contributed so much to our field success and brought in like-minded new friends. Although Hugh is pulled in more directions than I, we still manage a project or two together, the occasional ocean sailing getaway with a rum on the quarterdeck or horse trip in far Spain, Colorado, or Poncho Villa's Sierra Madre. It was Hugh's access to the Hiram Bingham archives and research at Yale during editing of *Lost Cities*

Hugh Thomson. Hugh Thomson photo.

of the Inca that led to our rediscovery of Bingham's misplaced, undocumented, and forgotten Llactapata.

John Hemming. Hugh Thomson photo.

John Hemming, recent past Director of the Royal Geographical Society, author of the definitive works, *The Conquest of the Incas* and *Monuments of the Incas*, has been our strongest supporter and advisor. John's confidence in us and our projects and his influential guidance led to grants and invaluable support from the RGS and other sources. John continues to advise, generously contributing suggestions, ideas, and information from his vast reserve of knowledge of the conquest and the Inca. Importantly, he has not hesitated to give critical review when we have strayed from the historical or archaeological record.

G. Ziegler photo.

Nick Asheshov, "experienced British explorer" earned the title as a surviving member of the ill-fated 1963 NGS expedition that parachuted into the far Vilcabamba, requiring an extensive and expensive rescue. As a first-line explorer-journalist, Nick has accumulated considerable knowledge of Andean cultures and seems to know everyone of consequence in Peru and around archaeological circles. Cambridge and Fleet Street trained, he was once publisher of the iconic English language newspaper, the *Lima Times*. He has been our behind-the-scenes mentor for obtaining needed government permits, while otherwise keeping us politically on track. As an owner, with wife Maria del Carmen, in the Machu Picchu railroad, Andean Railways, that originated at the Asheshov house in Urubamba, he supplied us with special trains, private rail service, and express resupply for work down the line to Machu Picchu and the terminus near Llactapata. Although hindered by near loss of vision, he has accompanied us on many demanding Vilcabamba explorations, "blindly leading us on" he would say.

Edwin Duenas. Larry Tracy photo.

Edwin Duenas is a highly valued member of our team. A Quechua-speaking Cusco native, Edwin practiced law with wife Fanny around the courts of Peru before catching the ancient mysteries bug. Edwin became our expedition Maestre del Campo, expertly organizing porters, camp staff, wranglers, and heading up logistical operations. He pursues ethnohistory with a passion. Edwin and Fanny are partners in our small Cusco-based educational travel, film support, and expeditions agency, Adventure Specialist Peru, which helps pay the bills. They own a family *chacra* near Cusco, where we keep our saddle horses and a place where I can hang my hat when in town. Each dry season we launch a new exploration together, dedicated to unraveling ancient Andean mysteries with the ongoing Andean Research Project.

Percy Paz. Edwin Duenas photo.

Percy Paz is the most deserving of credit and the least recognized of Vilcabamba explorers. He quietly, with dedicated efficiency, studied, explored, mapped, excavated, collected, and supervised a team of workers at Choquequirao over many years, while regularly making the difficult two-day trek in and out across the deep Apurimac gorge. As a Peruvian archaeologist working for a government agency, many of his papers, notes, and accumulated data have been unfortunately buried in agency files and some plagiarized by others. Percy shared his findings and thesis freely on the many occasions we have been together. Percy studied under John Rowe to become a leading authority on the Inca and period ceramics. Much of what we have learned about Choquequirao and its builders, a major portion of this writing, comes from his extensive fieldwork, insights, and investigations. Sadly, before Percy could read this book in its final form, he died in his home in Cusco in December of 2012.

John Leivers, inexhaustible Australian explorer, is the world's authority on remote Vilcabamba. There are few places that he has not been. Frequently

John Leivers. G. Ziegler photo.

traveling alone, he has compiled volumes of notebooks on undocumented sites throughout the immense drainages, cloud-forested ridges, and high peaks between the Urubamba and Apurimac Rivers. He has been shot, hunted by narco trafi-cantes, and nearly drowned in raging torrents. John has been our most valuable team leader. If a craggy hill needed exploring, John always led the team. As ocean rower Roz Savage said on the 2003 Llactapata expedition, "It would have been impenetrable vegetation except John just penetrated it." John is reported to be in the Australian Life Guard Hall of Fame. Among other noted adventures, he trekked solo from Colombia to Panama across the Darien Jungle. He has recently been featured in an adventure travel book entitled *Turn Right at Machu Picchu* as a sort of Andean Crocodile Dundee.

Paolo Greer. Lillian Roberts photo.

Paolo Greer, the quintessential Alaskan researcher, lives in the dark recesses of old libraries and dusty archives ever in search of ancient documents. In the field, Paolo meticulously records everything down to the distance from the cook tent to the latrine. It is always a pleasure when sorting through field notes at home to find that Paolo has just the photo and measurements for a feature that we missed. He contributes unfaltering energy and enthusiasm. It was his dedicated research that led to the uncovering of early intrigues at Machu Picchu before Hiram Bingham. His unmitigated generosity with research data has led to plagiarism of his work by less talented others. Paolo joined us on follow-up work at Llactapata, the 2006 expedition to survey Palcay, explorations in the Lucumayu drainage, and most recently at Choquequirao.

Tom Zuidema (l) and Gary Ziegler (r). John Leivers photo.

R. Tom Zuidema, the well-known Dutch ethnohistorian and world recognized authority on the Inca, critically reviewed our reports and work in the field. Tom brings a lifetime of accumulated insight, knowledge, and enhanced understanding of the Inca, early colonial writings, and ethnohistory—generously shared. His suggestions and observations have been a paramount contribution. Tom radiates inexhaustible energy and animated interest. I recall him fearlessly leading us up the sloping dome roof of the Santa Domingo Monastery in Cusco, high above the streets below to point out important *ceques* points on the horizon. Even as an experienced mountaineer, I was hesitant to follow him. On another occasion, we celebrated his eighty-first birthday in a high camp at Llactapata following an exhausting long day of cloud forest exploring. I learned more from Tom in a few weeks than during several years of grad school.

Vince Lee. Vince Lee photo.

Vince Lee is a Princeton-trained architect, former U.S. Marine, climber, explorer, rancher, film personality, and a world-renowned authority on Inca construction and site design. He is an intrepid Vilcabamba explorer and dedicated researcher. Remarkably, fellow Coloradan Vince and I have never worked in the field together, although we were both climbing guides in the Tetons at one time and have passed each other on several occasions in the Andes. We became fast friends and regular confidants over the years. Vince and Peru Peace Corps veteran, wife Nancy, are two of a handful of dedicated, tough explorer-researchers who have consistently braved the rugged Vilcabamba. Vince rates as the best informed of all. If you need a site plan or description of some remote Inca refuge, Vince has it professionally diagramed and will gladly share.

Barry Walker MBE, noted ornithologist and British Consul in Cusco, consistently made the logistics work for us. Barry is the acclaimed author of *The Birds of Machu Picchu*. It was in Barry's Cusco Cross Keys Pub many years ago that Barry inspired me to pursue the investigation of Choquequirao as the greatest remaining enigma of Vilcabamba. For many years, Barry was my business partner in an educational adventure tour operation, which paid the bills, allowing us to pursue our individual research agendas. The cook, camp staff, and drivers were always there when needed. We shared many good adventures together, perhaps the most memorable being the search for the Inca road we were convinced must have followed along the Apurimac to Choquequirao. We did not find the road, although we climbed from the river below to the glaciers above in the most rugged

G. Ziegler photo.

of terrain and conditions, finally to determine that it did not exist. However, we did find a large, likely *Chanca* settlement, an interesting group of round shaped ruins and cave burials in the Quebrada Abuela.

David Espejo. G. Ziegler photo.

David Espejo, Quechua-speaking Cusco native and expert on traditional Andean community customs, beliefs, and ceremonies has been a resourceful team leader, local liaison, and gifted discoverer of hidden sites. We worked together for several decades both in the Vilcabamba and at Chachapoyas. He is willing to drop everything when an advanced scout is needed to go in before or to head up a team. David works as an archaeology-specialist tour guide and has appeared in several Discovery film productions. We worked together some years ago on an Australian film fantasy centered on discovering a lost city in the Puncuyoc Range, which I helped write. I played the Hiram Bingham-like character and David played a shaman in traditional dress who points the way, consulting Pachamama and sacred mountain *apus*. It was a great adventure and we did actually discover an undocumented site.

Jorge Moreau and I organized our first expedition to Espiritu Pampa many years ago, which launched my archeo-explorer career. Jorge was working as head photographer and a writer for the Lima paper, *El Comercio*. Between classes at San Marcos and digs on the coast, I worked as a photographer for the paper with Jorge, attending embassy parties and conferences with Nikon and flash in hand. Jorge was soon involved in our archaeological studies and excavation sorties near Lima

G. Ziegler photo.

at the coastal ceremonial center, Pachacamac. When news hit the press about Gene Savoy's discoveries in Vilcabamba, we organized a small expedition backed by *El Comercio* to investigate. Arriving in Cusco, we obtained the backing and support of the Patronata de Arqueologia (see note 14). Jorge went on to become a well-known investigative journalist and a surviver of Argentina's bad, dangerous political years there. We lost contact when I returned home for army duties and new adventures in Vietnam. It was Jorge's dynamic energy, contacts, and friendship that helped set me on the Andean discovery road. Thanks to the Internet, we have reconnected. He and wife Silvia now live in Florida, having become proud new U.S. citizens.

Amy Finger and Gary Ziegler at Vitcos.
G. Ziegler photo.

Amy Finger came on board late, missing the early years in Vilcabamba, but became a moving inspiration and dedicated supporter of our projects. She is a knowledgeable Inca expert who has endured the hardships of the far Vilcabamba on a number of expeditions since the early 1990s. She is always there to help organize the next exploration and keep the finances on track. Amy frequently guides Adventure Specialists' archaeological horse tours and educational programs in the Sacred Valley, Machu Picchu, Argentina, and Spain. Meanwhile, she manages the home Colorado ranch base. She is author of a recently published, award-winning book, *Different Stokes for Different Folks.*

Frank Ciampa and I connected back in the mid-nineties. He had been with Gene Savoy on several epic expeditions, including Savoy's rediscovery of Gran Vilaya near Chachapoyas. I don't recall how we first communicated, but he was attending a military-related conference in Denver as a Marine Corps Chaplain. I drove to the big city to meet with him. We became friends and later planned out the 1997 expedition to visit Vilaya (see note 14). We found a large unknown site we humorously named Chachu Picchu. Frank and I returned again with a small expedition to Chachapoyas in 2011 and plan another exploration soon. Frank's wife is from there giving him a large, local extended family, an excellent resource for locating undocumented ruins. Having now retired from his military career, Frank has the interest, time, and resources to pursue the lost cities quest.

Frank Ciampa at Chachapoyas, 2011. G. Ziegler photo.

Deserving others to whom we owe our thanks and gratitude

Ken and Ruth Wright: From years of careful fieldwork they have each produced a definitive book on Machu Picchu, Ken's a careful, statistic-laden, valuable work on Inca engineering, and Ruth's the only really excellent guidebook to the site. They later published definitive books together on the water site, Tipon, and the enigmatic, enhanced sinkholes at Moray. The Wrights have generously shared their work and observations over the years. With dedication and passion for unraveling ancient mysteries, they continue intensive field investigations in the Inca heartland applying an unprecedented ability to reveal lost Inca secrets.

Peter Frost, Cusco-based travel writer, trek guide, and Inca documentary specialist joined me on several explorations some years ago, including the expedition to Chachapoyas in 1999 and the NGS Corihuayrachina project of 2001. He is unusually knowledgeable and an avid researcher. His insights have been helpful in making some of the interpretations of later years. I keep his excellent booklet, *Exploring Cusco*, handy as a simple, accurate source book when in need of a quick misplaced detail.

Robert Von Kaupp, Washington, D.C.-based American archaeologist, has generated volumes of hard-gained data and valuable information accumulated over several decades of rugged explorations and investigations around the Vilcabamba. Working with Peruvian colleagues, he documented and surveyed numbers of previously unknown sites. We communicated regularly. Bob generously sent unpublished reports of his projects, affording a valuable source for cross-referencing the Inca occupation of the region. Little known to the popular Inca studies world, Bob was one of a select group of unsung, dedicated explorers who have made major contributions to our understanding of this remote region and the last Inca. Sadly, news of Bob's passing arrived as of this writing.

Johan Reinhard, well-known American anthropologist, climber, and Explorer in Residence at the National Geographical Society, has located well-preserved mummies on high Andean peaks. His discovery of intact frozen bodies in Argentina and Peru has greatly advanced knowledge of Inca customs and diet. Johan has been helpful, supporting, and encouraging. He generously shared notes and reports on his early explorations of Inca routes and remote sites between Machu Picchu and Vitcos. He helped us immensely with the exploration of the Palcay region and outlying areas of Llactapata. His work on Machu Picchu as a sacred center strongly influenced our interpretations of Inca mountain ceremonial sites.

Finally, warm thanks and appreciation go out to those who have helped with funding, joined in on the fieldwork, and who otherwise gave support. From many years back, Jorge Muelle and La Universidad Nacional de San Marcos, *El Comercio*, The Royal Geographical Society, the BBC, Iain Stewart, The Explorers Club, Josh Bernstein, Mike Nowak and Colorado College, Brian Bauer, William Isbell, Luis Lumbreras, David Ugarte, the Instituto Nacional de Cultura, Gene Savoy, Pio Espinoza, Ramiro Abendanio, Aurelio Huaman, Hugo Peper, Mario Ortiz, David Guevara, Pepe Noriega, Gill Hazell, John Martin, Robert Mroczek, Jack Vetter, Roz Savage, Liz Nicol, Mark Davidson, Joan Harrell, Robert Hamilton, Linda Buczynski, Ann and Gary Bradley, Larry Tracy, Dan Kahler, Dean Shreve, Humberto Medrano, Greg Danforth, Kim MacQuarrie, Marcus Covert, Wyley Cotton, Catherine McGuire, Mitzi Adams, Dennis Gallagher, Mark Finger, Beth de Silva, Forrest Ketchin, and of course, Nancy Malville.

An additional special thanks goes to Paolo Greer, Hugh Thomson, Ruth and Ken Wright, Humberto Medrano, and Carlos Aranibar for photo contributions and other help. Hugh supplied several historic images from his early visit to Choquequirao. Humberto graciously photographed the June solstice sunrise at Choquequirao for us. John Hemming and Vince Lee contributed invaluable critical review and suggestions. The Wrights provided their excellent archaeological map of Machu Picchu and other important photos. Members of our most recent 2013 visit to Choquequirao: Steve Bein, Lillian Roberts, Ken Greenwood, Ken Mick, Joy Collins, and Amanda Stouffer contributed an immense selection of ultra-quality images to enhance the book, as well as helping with final site details and measurements.

Glossary of Quechua-Spanish

Exact translations of Quechua, the principal native language of the Andes, is difficult. There are many dialects, and meanings differ frequently from community to community. We have attempted to give the most accepted meanings. As Quechua was not a written language until translated phonetically into colonial period Spanish, it is frequently written in old and modern Spanish form. An attempt has been made to more closely spell words as they are pronounced. We have chosen to stay with modern Spanish form. Some relevant Spanish words are also included.

abra: Mountain pass.
acequia: Water channel ditch or canal.
alcalde: Mayor or chief community administrator.
andenes: Walled terraces or tiered platforms.
apachitas: Small stones carried up mountain passes and left in piles as spiritual offerings.
apu: An important Inca official, governor, or commander. It also refers to sacred geographical features, usually mountains, as spirits or deities.
Apurimac: Commonly defined as the speaking god river, probably because of the loud noise of the rapids. Rimac refers to speaking.
arriero: A wrangler who works with horses and mules.
axis mundi: A symbolic connection point between earth, sky, and the underworld.
ayllus: Kinship groups, traditionally two in Andean communities.
bamba: A flat or level area in the mountains, also called a *pampa*.
camac: The source or giver of spiritual empowerment.

camay: Spiritual empowerment of objects by the passage of water, sun, or other processes.

capac nan: A major Inca road several yards wide with retaining walls, bridges, and raised causeways over bogs; also called Inca *nan*.

Capac raymi: The important ceremonial events of the December solstice.

cancha: A stone-walled enclosure, usually rectangular, which may be a corral or contains one or more buildings.

caracas: Local administrators or chief of a community. There were traditionally two.

ceques: Imaginary lines radiating outward from a temple in a circle, believed to organize areas of labor, ritual responsibility, events and connect a network of shrines and huacas.

cerro: Spanish term for hill or mountain.

chacra: A farm or plot of agricultural land.

Chanca: An ethnic group and polity that preceeded Inca occupation of the central Andes north and west of Cusco. They were conquered or incorporated into the expanding Inca state.

Chachapoyas: A region in north-central Peru that was the homeland of an ethnic group and polity of the same name (*Chachapoya*), sometimes referred to as "the Cloud People."

chicha: An alcoholic beverage—beer made from corn used domestically and ceremonially.

Choquequirao: Reported to mean cradle of gold in Aymara, the southern Andean language spoken today around Lake Titicaca. However, many places in Vilcabamba are named Choque, which means hilltop or summit. The name likely refers to a peak of metal from the Quechua "quirao" for the nearby silver mines at Cerro Victoria.

coca: Leaves from a cultivated Andean shrub that were ceremonially used throughout the Andes and as a stimulant and medicinal plant. Todeay, cocaine is processed from coca.

colca: A building for storing food, weapons, tools, textiles, and other items.

conjunto: Group of buildings.

Coricancha: Enclosure of gold, the name of the principal sun temple in Cusco.

Corihuayrachina: Place where grain is thrashed. Cori refers to gold, in this case the color of grain.

Cotacoca: Lake of coca in Aymara, a southern Andean language spoken in parts of Bolivia and southern Peru.

cuy: Guinea pig.

encomienda: An early colonial land grant of a region, granting its population and resources to members of the original Spanish conquest.

espejado: "Like a mirror"—Spanish Andean phrase for a very clear day.

Espiritu Pampa: Plain of the spirits, location of the neo-Inca city Vilcabamba (La Vieja).

huaca: An Inca shrine, sacred place, or object.

Huaca Huilca: Sacred huaca; Quechua name for the ice peak, Veronica.

hanan: Upper half of a duel sociopolitical organization. It also refers to an upper partition of segmented Inca urban design.

hanan pacha: The spiritual world above.

huaquero: A treasure hunter who loots archaeological sites.

huaque: Brother, effigy, statue, or object representing the Inca.

Huayna Capac: Last Inca emperor before the civil wars and arrival of the Spanish.

hurin: Lower half of a duel sociopolitical organization. It also refers to a lower partition of segmented Inca urban design.

Hurincancha: Lower enclosure or compound, outlying group at Choquequirao.

Inca: Used to describe the entire polity or people, but also refers to the ruler, or Sapa Inca, individually.

Inca nan: A major Inca road several yards wide with retaining walls, bridges, and raised causeways over bogs; also called *capac nan*.

Inti: The sun.

intihuatana: Name given to similar, carved, upright stone projections at important Inca ceremonial sites.

intipunku: A sun gate, usually a tall stone entranceway with a double-jamb doorway.

Inti raymi: Ceremonial events and festivities during the June solstice.

llama: Andean camelid used for packing, wool, meat, and ceremonial sacrifice.

kallanca: A long, unpartitioned, narrow building with multiple entrances used as a meeting hall, for celebrations, or sometimes as a shrine.

kay pacha: The concept of the present—the here and now.

killke: Term used to describe early Inca sites and pottery before 1400 CE, usually referred to as transitional Inca.

Llactapata: A high city, place, or settlement.

Machu Picchu: Machu refers to old, picchu is commonly thought to mean peak, however the term also refers to a wad of coca in the mouth, which looks like a mound or hill.

machay: A cave or underground place.

masma: U-shaped structure.

mirador: Overlook or walled platform in a high place.

Mitimae, Mitayos: ethnic group settlers and workers resettled around the empire by the Inca administration to reduce rebellion, populate a region, or work specific projects with skilled workers.

moya: Water shrine usually associated with a royal estate.

neo-Inca: Remnant of the exiled Inca state and population that resisted colonial authorities until 1572.

Nusta Hispanan: The urinating place of an Inca princess, another name for the White Rock (Yuroc Rumi) shrine near Vitcos.

oroya: A cable stretched across a river or gorge with an attached box pulled back and forth with passengers and cargo.

Pachacuti: Earthshaker, name of the important Inca ruler. Pacha refers to earth.

Pachamama: Mother Earth.

pampa: A flat or level area in the mountains, or sometimes a vast region such as the Pampas of Argentina.

panaca: Royal Inca lineage group responsible for maintaining the properties and assets of a deceased Inca and his mummy.

Patawasi: High house.

pikiwasi: A house with biting flies.

Pinchaunuyoc: Place of water or a spring.

pirca: Crude fieldstone construction.

puna: High, cool country above timberline and below the glaciers.

quebrada: Canyon or gorge.

recinto: Long, sunken enclosure.

sacerdotes: Religious attendants or priests.

Salcantay: Highest peak near Machu Picchu and Choquequirao.

sapa (sapan) Inca: The highest authority, the ruling Inca.

Sendero Luminoso: Illuminated path; the name of the Andean Maoist-terrorist group.

suntarwasi: A constructed, ceremonial feature, usually a round platform or house with a tall pole pointing skyward, symbolically connecting the site with the heavens.

tambo: A way station on an Inca road, usually several houses, *colcas*, and sometimes a corral for llamas.

ucha pacha: The underworld.

usnu: A monument of stones or a leveled, raised-platform usually with retaining walls for observations, ceremonies, offerings, and perhaps signaling.

Usnu Capac: The central and most important ceremonial platform in Cusco.

Vilcabamba: Sacred plain, may come from the word wilka, meaning sacred. *Bamba* refers to a flat place, also called *pampa*.

Wasi: A house or building.

wayrona: A single room structure open on one side, usually at a ceremonial site.

yupanki: Inca title meaning honored or esteemed.

Yuroc Rumi: White rock; one of several names for the important Inca Shrine near Vitcos.

Bibliography

Alencastre Montufat, Gustavo. *Choqek'iraw, la Ciuidad de Los Condores.* Cultura y Pueblo, number 9–10, Lima, 1966.

Aveni, A. "Horizon Astronomy in Incaic Cusco" In *Archaeoastronomy in the Americas,* edited by R. Williamson, pp. 305–318. Balina Press, Los Altos, 1981.

___. "Archaeoastronomy in the Ancient Americas." In *Journal of Archaeological Research* 11:149–191, 2003.

Bauer, Brian. *The Development of the Inca State*, University of Texas Press, Austin, 1992.

___. *The Sacred Landscape of the Inca: The Cusco Ceque System.* University of Texas Press, Austin, 1998.

___. *Ancient Cuzco: Heartland of the Inca.* University of Texas Press, Austin, 2004.

Bauer, Brian, and David Dearborn. *Astronomy and Empire in the Ancient Andes: The Cultural Origins of Inca Sky Watching.* University of Texas Press, Austin, 1995.

Bauer, Brian, and Charles Stanish. *Ritual and Pilgrimage in the Ancient Andes: The Islands of the Sun and the Moon.* University of Texas Press, Austin, 2001.

Betanzos, Juan de. "Suma y Narracion de Los Incas" [1551]. *Biblioteca Peruana,* vol 3. E.T.A. Lima, 1968.

Bingham, Hiram. "The Ruins of Choquequirau." *American Anthropologist,* N.S.12, 1910.

___. "In the Wonderland of Peru." *National Geographic,* April, 1913.

___. *Lost City of the Incas.* Phoenix House, London, 1952. Revised edition with photos and Introduction by Hugh Thomson. Weidenfeld and Nicolson, London, 2002.

Bray, Tarmara. "An Archaeological Perspective on the Andean Concept of Camaquen: Thinking Through the Late Pre-Columbian

Ofrendas and Huacas. *Cambridge Archaeological Journal* 19, 357–366, 2009.

Burger, Richard. L. *Chavin and the Origins of Andean Civilization.* Thames and Hudson, London, 1992.

Burger, Richard L., and Lucy Salazar-Burger. "Machu Picchu Rediscovered: The Royal Estate in the Cloud Forest." *Discovery,* No. 24, 1993.

Burger, Richard L., edited by Lucy Salazar-Burger. "The 1912 Yale Peruvian Scientific Expedition Collections from Machu Picchu: Human and Animal Remains." *Yale University Publications in Anthropology,* No. 85, 2003.

Cabada Hildebrandt, Eulogio. (2008) *El Calendario Solar de Machu picchu y Otras Incognitas.* Lima, pp. 49–59.

Calancha, Antonio de la. *Coronica Moralizada del Orden de San Agustin en el Peru.* Barcelona, 1639.

Cieza de Lion, Pedro de. *La Cronica del Peru (tres partes).* Instituto de Estudias Peruanos, Lima, 1967.

Cobo, Bernabe. *History of the Inca Empire* [1633]. Translated by Roland Hamilton, University of Texas Press, Austin, 1983.

COPESCO. Proyecto de Restauracion Y Puesto En Valor Del Conjunto Archeologico De Choquequirao. Vol. 1, 1987.

Couture, N.C. "Monumental Space, Courtly Style, and Elite Life at Tiwanaku." In *Tiwanaku: Ancestors of the Inca,* edited by M. Young-Sanchez. University of Nebraska Press, Lincoln, 2004.

Cummins, T. "The Felicitous Legacy of the Lanzón." In *Chavín: Art Architecture and Culture,* edited by W.J. Conklin and J. Quilter, pp. 279. University of Nebraska Press, Lincoln, 2004.

D'Altroy, Terence. *The Incas.* Blackwell Publishing, London, 2003.

Dean, C. *A Culture of Stone.* Duke University Press, Durham, NC, 2010.

Dearborn, David. *"Archaeoastronomy in the Americas."* Ballena Press anthropological papers no. 22. Los Altos, 1981.

Dearborn, David S. P., and Raymond E. White. "Inca Observatories: Their Relation to the Calendar and Ritual." In *World Archaeoastronomy,* edited by A.F. Aveni, pp.462–469. Cambridge University Press, Cambridge, 1989.

Dearborn, David, and Katherine Schreiber. "Here Comes the Sun: The Cusco–Machu Picchu Connection." *Archaeoastronomy*, IX:15–36, 1986.

Dearborn, David, Matthew Seddon, and Brian Bauer. "The Sanctuary of Titicaca: Where the Sun Returns to Earth." *Latin American Antiquity* 9, 3:240-258, 1998.

Dearborn, David, and Raymond White. "The 'Torreon' at Machu Picchu as an Observatory." *Archaeoastronomy* 5, Supplement of the *Journal for History of Astronomy*, S37–S49, 1983.

Dearborn, David, Katharine Schreiber D.S., and Raymond White. "Intimachay: A December Solstice Observatory at Machu Picchu, Peru." *American Antiquity* 52 (2):346–352, 1987.

Drew, David. *The Cusichaca Project: The Lucumayo and Santa Teresa Valleys.* British Archaeological Reports, International Series 210, Oxford, 1984.

Duffait, Erwan. "Choquequirao en el siglo XVI: etnohistoria e implicaciones arqueologicas." *Bulletin de L'Institut d'Etudes Andines* 34:185–196, 2005.

Eliade, Mircea. *Shamanism: Archaic Techniques of Ecstasy.* Princeton University Press, Princeton, 1964.

Farrington, I. S. "The Mummy, Estate, and the Palace of Inka Huayna Capac at Quispenguanca." *Tawantinsuyu* 1:55, 1995.

Fejos, Paul. "Archaeological Explorations in the Cordillera Vilcabamba Peru." Viking Fund, Number 3, New York, 1944.

Fritz, John. "Paleopsychology Today: Ideational Systems and Human Adaption in Prehistory." In *Social Anthropology: Beyond Subsistence and Dating*, edited by C. L. Redman et al., pp. 37–59. Academic Press, New York, 1978.

Garcilaso de la Vega, Inca. *Royal Commentaries of the Incas and General History of Peru 1604.* Translated by H.V. Livermore, University of Texas Press, Austin, 1987.

Gasparini, Graziano and Luise Margolies. *Inca Architecture.* Translated by Patricia Lyon. Indiana University Press, Bloomington, 1980.

Ghezzi I. "Religious Warfare at Chankillo." In *Andean Archaeology*

III: North and South, edited by W.H. Isbell and H. Silverman, pp. 67–84. Springer, New York, 2006.

Ghezzi I, and C. Ruggles. "Chankillo: A 2300-Year-Old Solar Observatory in Coastal Peru." In *Science* 315:1239–1243, 2007.

___. "The Social and Ritual Context of Horizon Astronomical Observations at Chankillo." In *Archaeoastronomy and Ethnoastronomy: Building Bridges Between Cultures,* edited by C. Ruggles, pp. 144–153. Cambridge University Press, Cambridge, 2011.

Gonzales Carre, Enrique. *Los Senorios Chankas.* Instituto Andino de Estudios Arqueologicos, Lima, 1994.

Gow, David. *Taytacha Qoyllur Rit'I: Rocas y bailarines, cruncias y continuidad.* Allpanchis, 1974.

Greer, Paolo. "Machu Picchu: A Revised History of Discovery." *South American Explorer,* Volume 87, 2008.

Guaman Poma de Alaya, Felipe. "Nueva Coronica y buen Gobierno." *Travaux et Memories de L'Institut d'Ethnologie,* 22. Paris, 1936.

Gullberg, Steve. "Inca Solar Orientations in Southeastern Peru." *Journal of Cosmology* 9:2078–2091, 2010.

Gullberg, Steve, and J. McKim Malville. "The Astronomy of Peruvian Huacas." In Orchiston, W., Nakamura, T., and Strom, R. (eds.). *Highlighting the History of Astronomy in the Asia-Pacific Region,* 85–118. Springer, New York, 2011.

Haas, J., and W. Creamer. "Crucible of Andean Civilization: The Peruvian Coast from 3000 to 1800 BC. In *Current Anthropology* 47:745–775, 2006.

___. "Why Do People Build Monuments? Late Archaic Platform Mounds in the Norte Chico." In *Early New World Monumentality,* edited by R.L. Burger and R.M. Rosenswig, pp. 289–312. University of Florida Press, 2012.

Hemming, John. *The Conquest of the Incas.* Revised edition. Pan Macmillan, London, 1993.

Hemming, John, and Edward Ranney. *Monuments of the Incas.* Revised edition. Thames and Hudson, New York and London, 2010.

Hyslop, John. *The Inca Road System.* Academic Press, New York, 1984.

___. *Inkawasi, The New Cuzco.* Institute of Andean Research, New York, 1985.

___. *Inka Settlement Planning.* University of Texas Press, Austin, 1990.

Kendall, Ann. *Aspects of Inca Architecture: Description, Function and Chronology,* 2 Volumes. British Archaeological Reports, International Series 210. Oxford, 1984.

___. "Inca planning north of Cuzco between Anta and Machu Picchu and along the Urubamba Valley." In Nicholas J. Saunders and Olivier de Montmollin (eds.), *Recent Studies in Pre-Columbian Archaeology*. B.A.R 421, Oxford, 1988.

Lee, Vincent. *Chanasuyu: Ruins of Inca Vilcabamba Sixpac Manco.* Wilson, 1989.

___. "Choqek'iraw: Inca Site Revealed." *South American Explorer,* Vol. 51, 1998.

___. *Forgotten Vilcabamba: Final Stronghold of the Inca.* Empire Publishing, 2000.

Lumbreras, Luis G. "Arqueologia de la America Andina." Editorial Miles Barnes. Lima, 1981.

Lumbreras, Luis G. and W. Wust. "Choquequirao: santuario historico y ecologico." Fundacion Telefonica, Lima, 2001.

MacQuarrie, Kim. *The Last Days of the Inca.* Simon & Schuster, New York, 2007.

Malville, J. McKim. "Animating the Inanimate: Camay and Astronomical Huacas of Peru." In Rubino-Martin, JoseA., Juan A. Belmonte, F. Prada, A. Alberdi (eds), *Astronomy Across Cultures.* Astronomical Society of the Pacific Conference Series, San Francisco, pp. 261–266, 2009.

___. "Cosmology in the Inca Empire: Huaca Sanctuaries, State Supported Pilgrimage, and Astronomy." *Journal of Cosmology* 9:2006–2020, 2010.

Malville, J. McKim, Hugh Thomson, and Gary Ziegler. "El Observatorio de Machu Picchu: Redescubrimiento de Llactapata y su templo solar." *Revista Andina* 39: 9–40. Cusco, 2004.

___. "The Sun Temple of Llactapata and the Ceremonial Neighborhood of Machu Picchu"; "Viewing the Sky Through Past and Present Cultures." Selected papers from the Oxford VII Conference on Archaeoastronomy. Pueblo Grande Museum Anthropological Papers No.15, Phoenix, 2006.

Malville J. McKim, Michael Zawaski, and Steven Gullberg. "Cosmological Motifs of Peruvian Huacas." *Archaeologia Baltica* 10:175–182, 2009.

Markham, Clements. *The Inca of Peru.* AMS Press, New York, 1910.

Moseley, Michael. *The Incas And Their Ancestors.* Thames and Hudson, New York and London, 1993.

Niles, Susan. *The Shape of Inca History.* University of Iowa Press. Iowa City, 1999.

Paternosto, C. *The Stone and the Thread: Andean Roots of Abstract Art.* University of Texas Press, Austin, 1989.

Paz, Flores, M. Pércy. "Ceremonias y Pinturas Rupestres. En Llamichos y Paqocheros: pastores de llamas y alpacas. Compilador Jorge A. Flores Ochoa. Edición: Centro de Estudios Andinos Cuzco, pp. 217–223. CEAS, Cusco, 1988.

___. "Llamaoq Anden, Los muros decorativos de Choquequirao." COPESCO, Cusco, 2004.

Pizarro, Pedro. "Relacion de 1565." Fondo Editorial, Universidad Catolica, Lima, 1987.

Poma de Ayala, Guaman. "La Nueva Cronica y buen gobierno." Vol. I, *Editorial Cultural*, Lima, 1956 [1613].

Prescott, William H. *History of the Conquest of Peru.* E.P. Dutton, New York, 1847.

Protzen, Jean-Pierre. *Inca Architecture and Construction at Ollantaytambo.* Oxford University Press, Oxford, 1993.

Ocampo, Baltasar de [1907]. Translated by C .Markham. "Account of the Province of Vilcabamba and a Narrative of the Execution of the Inca Tupac Amaru." Hakluyt Society, Ser. 2, Vol. 23:203–47, Cambridge.

Reinhard, Johan. "Informe sobre una sección del camino Inca y las ruinas en la cresta que baja del nevado de Tucarhuay entre los ríos Aobamba y Santa Teresa." *Revista Sacsahuaman,* No. 3:163–187, Cusco, 1990.

___. *Machu Picchu, The Sacred Center.* Instituto Machu Picchu, Cusco, 2002.

___. *Machu Picchu: Exploring an Ancient Sacred Center.* 4th ed. Cotsen Institute of Archaeology, Los Angeles, 2007.

RGI. *Relaciones Geographicas de Indias.* 3 volumes, Bilioteca de Autores, Vols. 183–185. Ediciones Atlas, Madrid, 1557–86.

Romero, Carlos A. "Informe sobre las ruinas de Choquequirao," *Rivista Historica,* Organo del Instituto Historico del Peru. Vol. 2, 1907.

Rostworowski, Maria. *Estructuras Andinas de Poder.* Instituto de Estudios Peruanos, Lima, 1983.

Rowe, John H. "Machu Picchu a la luz de documentos del siglo XVI." *Historia* 16 (1):139–154, Lima,1990.

___. "An Introduction to the Archaeology of Cusco." Papers of the Peabody Museum Vol. 27, No. 2, Harvard University Press, 1994.

Salomon, F., and G.L. Urioste. *The Huarochiri Manuscript: A Testament of Ancient and Colonial Andean Religion.* University of Texas Press, Austin, 1991.

Samanez Argumedo, Roberto, and Julio Zapata Rodriguez."El Conjunto Arqueologico Inka De Choquequirao Andes: Revista de la Facultad de Ciencias Sociales." Sem. 94 II, Universidad Nacional de San Antonio Abad, Cusco, 1995.

___. "La Casa de la Caida del Agua: vivienda del Inca de Choquequirao." *Arkinka,* No. 92, Lima, 2003.

Savoy, Gene. *Antisuyo, The Search for the Lost Cities of the Amazon.* Simon & Schuster, New York, 1970.

Solis, Ruth Shady. "America's First City? The Case of Late Archaic Caral." In *Andean Archaeology* III: North and South, edited by Willliam H. Isbell and Helaine Silverman, pp. 28–66. Springer, New York, 2006.

Squier, E.G. *Peru: Incidents of Travel and Exploration in the Land of the Incas.* Harper Brothers, New York, 1877.

Staller, John. E., ed. "Dimensions of Place: The Significance of Centers to the Development of Andean Civilization: An Exploration of the Ushnu Concept." In *Pre-Columbian Landscapes of Creation and Origin*, pp. 269–313. Springer, New York, 2008.

Thomson, Hugh. *The White Rock: An Exploration of the Inca Heartland.* Orion, London, 2001.

___. *A Sacred Landscape: The Search for Ancient Peru.* Overlook, New York, 2006.

Thomson, Hugh, and Gary Ziegler. Cotacoca Reconnaissance Expedition Report, 2002. http://www.thomson.clara.net/cotacoca.html.

Titu Cusi Yupanqui [1570]. "Relacion de la Conquista del Peru y Hechos del Inca Manco II." Carlos Romero and Horacio Urteaga, Coleccion de libros y documentos referentes a la historia del Peru, Series 1, vol 2, Lima, 1916.

Urton, Gary. *At the Crossroads of the Earth and Sky, An Andean Cosmology.* University of Texas Press, Austin, 1981.

___. *The History of a Myth: Pacariqtambo and the Origin of the Inkas.* University of Texas Press, Austin, 1990.

Van deGutche, M. "Carving the World: Inca Monumental Sculpture and Landscape." Ph.D dissertation, University of Illinois, Urbana-Champaign, 1990.

Villanueva, Urteaga Horacio. "Cuzco 1689: Economía y sociedad en el sur andino." Con prefacio de Pablo Macera. Edición Centro de Estudios Andinos Bartolomé de las Casas, Cusco, 1982.

Von Kaupp, Robert. "Reconocimiento Arqueologico en la region de Vilcabamba." Self published, personal communication, 2002.

Von Kaupp, Robert, and Octavio Fernandez Carrasco. "Vilcabamba Disconecida." Self published, Lima, 2010.

Westerman, James. S. "Inti, the Condor and the Underworld: The Archaeoastronomical Implications of the Newly Discovered Caves at Machu Picchu, Peru." In Fountain, J. W., and R. M. Sinclair (eds.), *Current Studies in Archaeoastronomy: Conversations Across Time and Space*, pp. 339–351. Carolina Academic Press, Durham, 2005.

White, Stuart. "Preliminary Site Survey of the Punkuyoq Range, Southern Peru." Papers of the Institute of Andean Studies, number 22–23, Berkeley, 1985.

Wright, Kenneth. *Machu Picchu, A Civil Engineering Marvel.* ASCE Press, Virginia, 2000.

Wright, Kenneth, and Ruth Wright. *Tipon: Water Engineering Masterpiece of the Inca Empire.* ASCE Press, Virginia, 2006.

Wright, Kenneth, and Ruth Wright, et al. *Moray: Inca Engineering Mystery.* ASCE Press, Virginia, 2011.

Wright, Ruth, and Dr. Alfredo Valencia Zegarra. *The Machu Picchu Guidebook: A Self-Guided Tour.* Johnson Books, Boulder, 2001.

Zawaski, Michael, and J. McKim Malville. "An Archaeoastronomical Survey of Major Inca Sites in Peru." *Archaeoastronomy: The Journal of Astronomy in Culture,* XXI:20–38, 2010.

Ziegler, Gary. "Vilcabamba, Report from the Field." *South American Explorer,* Vol. 57, 1999.

___. *Beyond Machu Picchu: Exploration and Adventure in Peru's Remote Vilcabamba.* Crestone Press, Westcliffe, 2001.

___. "Corihuayrachina, Victoria's Secret Revealed: A Preliminary Report of the 2001 National Geographic Society Vilcabamba Expedition." Web published, 2002, www.adventurespecialists.org/victoria_report.html

___. "Palcay, an Almost Lost City and Other Explorations." *South American Explorer,* Vol. 84, 2007.

Ziegler, Gary, and Hugh Thomson. "The Cotacoca Reconnaissance Project." Royal Geographical Society. Web published, 2002, www.adventurespecialists.org/cotareport.html.

Ziegler, Gary, and J. McKim Malville. "Machu Picchu, Inca Pachacuti's Sacred City: A Multiple Ritual, Ceremonial and Administrative Center. Web published, 2006, www.adventurespecialists.org/mapi1.html

___. "Choquequirao, Topa Inca's Machu Picchu: a royal estate and ceremonial center." In *Archaeoastronomy and Ethnoastronomy: Building Bridges between Cultures, Oxford IX International Symposium on Archaeoastronomy*, edited by Clive Ruggles, pp. 154–161. Cambridge: Cambridge University Press, 2011.

Ziólkowski M., Kosciuk J., and Victoria F. Astete. "Astronomical Observations at Intimachay (Machu Picchu): A New Approach to an Old Problem." In *Ancient Cosmologies and Modern Prophets,* edited by I. Sprajc and P. Pehani. Proceedings of the 20th Conference of the European Society of Astronomy in Culture. Slovene Anthropological Society Ljubljana, pp. 391–404, 2013.

Zuidema, R. Tom. *The Ceque System of Cuzco: The Social Organization of the Capital of the Inca.* E. J. Brill, Leiden, 1964.

___. "Shaft Tombs and the Inca Empire." *Journal of the Steward Anthropological Society* 28:317–361, 1978.

___. "Catachillay: The Role of the Pleiades and of the Southern Cross and a and b Centeauri in the Calendar of the Incas." *Annals of the New York Academy of Sciences,* 385:203–229, 1982.

___. *La Civilisation Inca en Cusco.* Paris, 1986. Translated by Jean-Jacques Decoster, Austin, 1991.

Index

Page numbers in **bold** indicate illustrations.

About the Authors

Gary Ziegler started his archaeological adventures and studies in Peru some decades ago when he organized his first expedition to Espiritu Pampa as a very young grad student at Peru's San Marcos University. Since then, he has pursued several different lives but always returns periodically to the Andes in search of mysteries to solve and to savor the adventure.

Dr. J. McKim Malville has taught in the astronomy departments of the universities of Michigan, Colorado, Sao Paulo, and James Cook in Townsville, Australia. He is presently professor emeritus in the Department of Astrophysical and Planetary Sciences at the University of Colorado. In addition to working in Peru, he has investigated archaeoastronomy in India, Egypt, and the American Southwest.